OECD/G20 Base Erosion and Profit Shifting Project

Designing Effective Controlled Foreign Company Rules, Action 3 - 2015 Final Report

Please cite this publication as:
OECD (2015), *Designing Effective Controlled Foreign Company Rules, Action 3 - 2015 Final Report*, OECD/G20 Base Erosion and Profit Shifting Project, OECD Publishing, Paris.
http://dx.doi.org/10.1787/9789264241152-en

ISBN 978-92-64-24114-5 (print)
ISBN 978-92-64-24115-2 (PDF)

Series: OECD/G20 Base Erosion and Profit Shifting Project
ISSN 2313-2604 (print)
ISSN 2313-2612 (online)

Photo credits: Cover © ninog – Fotolia.com

Corrigenda to OECD publications may be found on line at: *www.oecd.org/about/publishing/corrigenda.htm*.

Foreword

International tax issues have never been as high on the political agenda as they are today. The integration of national economies and markets has increased substantially in recent years, putting a strain on the international tax rules, which were designed more than a century ago. Weaknesses in the current rules create opportunities for base erosion and profit shifting (BEPS), requiring bold moves by policy makers to restore confidence in the system and ensure that profits are taxed where economic activities take place and value is created.

Following the release of the report *Addressing Base Erosion and Profit Shifting* in February 2013, OECD and G20 countries adopted a 15-point Action Plan to address BEPS in September 2013. The Action Plan identified 15 actions along three key pillars: introducing coherence in the domestic rules that affect cross-border activities, reinforcing substance requirements in the existing international standards, and improving transparency as well as certainty.

Since then, all G20 and OECD countries have worked on an equal footing and the European Commission also provided its views throughout the BEPS project. Developing countries have been engaged extensively via a number of different mechanisms, including direct participation in the Committee on Fiscal Affairs. In addition, regional tax organisations such as the African Tax Administration Forum, the *Centre de rencontre des administrations fiscales* and the *Centro Interamericano de Administraciones Tributarias*, joined international organisations such as the International Monetary Fund, the World Bank and the United Nations, in contributing to the work. Stakeholders have been consulted at length: in total, the BEPS project received more than 1 400 submissions from industry, advisers, NGOs and academics. Fourteen public consultations were held, streamed live on line, as were webcasts where the OECD Secretariat periodically updated the public and answered questions.

After two years of work, the 15 actions have now been completed. All the different outputs, including those delivered in an interim form in 2014, have been consolidated into a comprehensive package. The BEPS package of measures represents the first substantial renovation of the international tax rules in almost a century. Once the new measures become applicable, it is expected that profits will be reported where the economic activities that generate them are carried out and where value is created. BEPS planning strategies that rely on outdated rules or on poorly co-ordinated domestic measures will be rendered ineffective.

Implementation therefore becomes key at this stage. The BEPS package is designed to be implemented via changes in domestic law and practices, and via treaty provisions, with negotiations for a multilateral instrument under way and expected to be finalised in 2016. OECD and G20 countries have also agreed to continue to work together to ensure a consistent and co-ordinated implementation of the BEPS recommendations. Globalisation requires that global solutions and a global dialogue be established which go beyond OECD and G20 countries. To further this objective, in 2016 OECD and G20 countries will conceive an inclusive framework for monitoring, with all interested countries participating on an equal footing.

A better understanding of how the BEPS recommendations are implemented in practice could reduce misunderstandings and disputes between governments. Greater focus on implementation and tax administration should therefore be mutually beneficial to governments and business. Proposed improvements to data and analysis will help support ongoing evaluation of the quantitative impact of BEPS, as well as evaluating the impact of the countermeasures developed under the BEPS Project.

Table of contents

Executive summary **9**

Introduction **11**

***Chapter 1* Policy considerations and objectives** **13**

1.1 Shared policy considerations 13
1.2 Specific policy objectives 15

***Chapter 2* Rules for defining a CFC** **21**

2.1 Recommendations 21
2.2 Explanation 21

***Chapter 3* CFC exemptions and threshold requirements** **33**

3.1 Recommendations 33
3.2 Explanation 33

***Chapter 4* Definition of CFC income** **43**

4.1 Recommendation 43
4.2 Explanation 43

***Chapter 5* Rules for computing income** **57**

5.1 Recommendations 57
5.2 Explanation 57

***Chapter 6* Rules for attributing income** **61**

6.1 Recommendations 61
6.2 Explanation 61

***Chapter 7* Rules to prevent or eliminate double taxation** **65**

7.1 Recommendations 65
7.2 Explanation 66

Figures

Figure 2.1 Modified hybrid mismatch rule 23
Figure 2.2 Control interest held by unrelated parties acting in concert 26
Figure 2.3 Control interest held by related parties 27
Figure 2.4 Calculation of indirect control interest 29
Figure 3.1 De minimis test 35
Figure 5.1 Loss limitation 58
Figure 5.2 Loss limitation with pre-existing passive limitation 59
Figure 7.1 Interaction of CFC rules 67

Abbreviation and acronyms

BEPS	Base erosion and profit shifting
CFA	Committee on Fiscal Affairs
CFC	Controlled foreign companies
ECJ	European Court of Justice
EEA	European Economic Area
ETR	Effective tax rate
FBE	Foreign Business Establishment
IFRS	International Financial Reporting Standards
IP	Intellectual Property
MNC	Multinational corporation
MNE	Multinational enterprise
OECD	Organisation for Economic Co-operation and Development
PE	Permanent establishment
R&D	Research and Development
SGI	Société de Gestion Industrielle
UK	United Kingdom
US	United States

Executive summary

Controlled foreign company (CFC) rules respond to the risk that taxpayers with a controlling interest in a foreign subsidiary can strip the base of their country of residence and, in some cases, other countries by shifting income into a CFC. Without such rules, CFCs provide opportunities for profit shifting and long-term deferral of taxation.

Since the first CFC rules were enacted in 1962, an increasing number of jurisdictions have implemented these rules. Currently, 30 of the countries participating in the OECD/G20 Base Erosion and Profit Shifting (BEPS) Project have CFC rules, and many others have expressed interest in implementing them. However, existing CFC rules have often not kept pace with changes in the international business environment, and many of them have design features that do not tackle BEPS effectively.

In response to the challenges faced by existing CFC rules, the *Action Plan on Base Erosion and Profit Shifting* (BEPS Action Plan, OECD, 2013) called for the development of recommendations regarding the design of CFC rules. This is an area where the OECD has not done significant work in the past, and this report recognises that by working together countries can address concerns about competiveness and level the playing field.

This report sets out recommendations in the form of building blocks. These recommendations are not minimum standards, but they are designed to ensure that jurisdictions that choose to implement them will have rules that effectively prevent taxpayers from shifting income into foreign subsidiaries. The report sets out the following six building blocks for the design of effective CFC rules:

- **Definition of a CFC** – CFC rules generally apply to foreign companies that are controlled by shareholders in the parent jurisdiction. The report sets out recommendations on how to determine when shareholders have sufficient influence over a foreign company for that company to be a CFC. It also provides recommendations on how non-corporate entities and their income should be brought within CFC rules.
- **CFC exemptions and threshold requirements** – Existing CFC rules often only apply after the application of provisions such as tax rate exemptions, anti-avoidance requirements, and *de minimis* thresholds. The report recommends that CFC rules only apply to controlled foreign companies that are subject to effective tax rates that are meaningfully lower than those applied in the parent jurisdiction.
- **Definition of income** – Although some countries' existing CFC rules treat all the income of a CFC as "CFC income" that is attributed to shareholders in the parent jurisdiction, many CFC rules only apply to certain types of income. The report recommends that CFC rules include a definition of CFC income, and it sets out a non-exhaustive list of approaches or combination of approaches that CFC rules could use for such a definition.

- **Computation of income** – The report recommends that CFC rules use the rules of the parent jurisdiction to compute the CFC income to be attributed to shareholders. It also recommends that CFC losses should only be offset against the profits of the same CFC or other CFCs in the same jurisdiction.

- **Attribution of income** – The report recommends that, when possible, the attribution threshold should be tied to the control threshold and that the amount of income to be attributed should be calculated by reference to the proportionate ownership or influence.

- **Prevention and elimination of double taxation** – One of the fundamental policy issues to consider when designing effective CFC rules is how to ensure that these rules do not lead to double taxation. The report therefore emphasises the importance of both preventing and eliminating double taxation, and it recommends, for example, that jurisdictions with CFC rules allow a credit for foreign taxes actually paid, including any tax assessed on intermediate parent companies under a CFC regime. It also recommends that countries consider relief from double taxation on dividends on, and gains arising from the disposal of, CFC shares where the income of the CFC has previously been subject to taxation under a CFC regime.

Because each country prioritises policy objectives differently, the recommendations provide flexibility to implement CFC rules that combat BEPS in a manner consistent with the policy objectives of the overall tax system and the international legal obligations of the country concerned. In particular, this report recognises that the recommendations must be sufficiently adaptable to comply with EU law, and it sets out possible design options that could be implemented by EU Member States. Once implemented, the recommendations will ensure that countries will have effective CFC rules that address BEPS concerns.

Introduction

1. Action 3 of the *Action Plan on Base Erosion and Profit Shifting* (BEPS Action Plan, OECD, 2013) recognises that groups can create non-resident affiliates to which they shift income and that these affiliates may be established wholly or partly for tax reasons rather than for non-tax business reasons.[1] Controlled foreign company (CFC) and other anti-deferral rules combat this by enabling jurisdictions to tax income earned by foreign subsidiaries where certain conditions are met. However, some countries do not currently have CFC rules and others have rules that do not always counter BEPS situations in a comprehensive manner. Action 3 calls for the development of "recommendations regarding the design of controlled foreign company rules". The objective was to develop recommendations for CFC rules that are effective in dealing with base erosion and profit shifting.

2. CFC rules have existed in the international tax context for over five decades, and dozens of countries have implemented these rules. This report considers all the constituent elements of CFC rules and breaks them down into the "building blocks" that are necessary for effective CFC rules. These building blocks would allow countries without CFC rules to implement recommended rules directly and countries with existing CFC rules to modify their rules to align more closely with the recommendations, and they include:

1. Rules for defining a CFC (including definition of control)
2. CFC exemptions and threshold requirements
3. Definition of CFC income
4. Rules for computing income
5. Rules for attributing income
6. Rules to prevent or eliminate double taxation.

3. Before discussing these six building blocks, this report first addresses the policy considerations to be considered in the context of Action 3. These include shared policy considerations that all jurisdictions consider when designing CFC rules as well as different policy objectives that are linked to the overall domestic tax systems of individual jurisdictions. Shared policy considerations include the role of CFC rules as a deterrent measure; how CFC rules complement transfer pricing rules; the need to balance effectiveness with reducing administrative and compliance burdens; and the need to balance effectiveness with preventing or eliminating double taxation. When addressing these policy considerations, jurisdictions prioritise their policy objectives differently depending, in part, on whether they have worldwide or territorial tax systems[2] and whether they are Member States of the European Union. These policy issues are all briefly considered in Chapter 1. The following chapters then set out the building blocks. The recommendations discussed in this report are designed to combat base erosion and

profit shifting. It is recognised that some countries are concerned about long-term deferral and that recommendations need to provide sufficient flexibility so that jurisdictions can design CFC rules that combat BEPS in a way that is consistent with both their international legal obligations and the policy objectives of their domestic tax systems.

4. The work on CFCs is being co-ordinated with the work on other Actions, including Action 1 (Addressing the tax challenges of the digital economy), Action 2 (hybrid mismatch arrangements), Action 4 (Interest deductions), Action 5 (Countering harmful tax practices), and Actions 8-10 (Transfer pricing).

Notes

1. Non-tax business reasons could include, for example, the availability of employees, increased resources, or a more favourable legal environment. CFC rules are not by definition limited to situations where CFCs are controlled by companies, and jurisdictions should consider designing CFC rules to apply in situations where individuals control foreign entities.
2. In reality, jurisdictions' tax systems are almost never purely worldwide nor purely territorial but fall within a spectrum between these two.

Bibliography

OECD (2013), *Action Plan on Base Erosion and Profit Shifting*, OECD Publishing, Paris, http://dx.doi.org/10.1787/9789264202719-en.

Chapter 1

Policy considerations and objectives

5. This chapter sets out a high level policy framework for CFC rules. Because CFC rules fit within a jurisdiction's overall system of tax, the design and objectives of CFC rules can differ from one jurisdiction to another because they reflect different policy choices. The chapter therefore first introduces the policy considerations that underlie all CFC rules and then lists several policy objectives that jurisdictions may prioritise differently.

1.1 Shared policy considerations

6. Depending on their design, CFC rules tax parent companies based on some or all of the income of some or all of their foreign subsidiaries. For most countries, they are used to prevent shifting of income either from the parent jurisdiction or from the parent and other tax jurisdictions. However, countries could also be concerned about long-term deferral. All CFC rules share some general policy considerations, including (i) their role as a deterrent measure; (ii) how they complement transfer pricing rules; (iii) the need to balance effectiveness with reducing administrative and compliance burdens; and (iv) the need to balance effectiveness with preventing or eliminating double taxation.

1.1.1 Deterrent effect

7. CFC rules are generally designed to act as a deterrent. In other words, CFC rules are not primarily designed to raise tax on the income of the CFC. Instead, they are designed to protect revenue by ensuring profits remain within the tax base of the parent or, in the case of CFC regimes that also target the stripping of third countries' bases ("foreign-to-foreign stripping"), other group companies, typically by preventing taxpayers from shifting income into CFCs. CFC rules will, of course, raise some revenue by taxing the income of CFCs, but there is likely to be a reduction in the income shifted to CFCs after the implementation of CFC rules. In common with other rules designed to change taxpayer behaviour, CFC rules may not exclusively have the effect that their design suggests. For example, the design of CFC rules suggests that they grant secondary taxing rights to the residence jurisdiction. In reality, however, if CFC rules effectively tax profits at a sufficiently high rate, they may also increase taxing opportunities in source jurisdictions by reducing or eliminating the tax incentives for multi-national enterprises (MNEs) to shift income into subsidiaries in low-tax jurisdictions.

1.1.2 Interaction with transfer pricing rules

8. Transfer pricing rules are intended to adjust the taxable profits of associated enterprises to eliminate distortions arising whenever the prices or other conditions of transactions between those enterprises differ from what they would have been if the enterprises had been unrelated. Because controlled foreign company rules by definition address related parties (as the companies that are captured by such rules are controlled by another party), jurisdictions often also use these rules to combat the adjusted prices charged between related parties. In other words, CFC rules are seen as a way for a parent jurisdiction to capture income earned by a foreign subsidiary that may not have been earned had the original pricing of the income-creating asset been set correctly. CFC rules are thus often referred to as "backstops" to transfer pricing rules.[1] That terminology, however, is misleading, in that CFC rules do not always complement transfer pricing rules. CFC rules may target the same income as transfer pricing rules in some situations, but it is unlikely that either CFC rules or transfer pricing rules in practice eliminate the need for the other set of rules. Instead, while CFC rules may capture some income that is not captured by transfer pricing rules (and vice versa), neither set of rules fully captures the income that the other set of rules intends to capture.

9. Transfer pricing rules, which generally rely on a facts and circumstances analysis and focus primarily on payments between related parties, do not remove the need for CFC rules. CFC rules are generally more mechanical and more targeted than transfer pricing rules, and many CFC rules automatically attribute certain categories of income that is more likely to be geographically mobile and therefore easy to shift into a low-tax foreign jurisdiction, regardless of whether the income was earned from a related party. CFC rules therefore play a unique role in the international tax system. Transfer pricing rules should generally apply before CFC rules, but even after the completion of the BEPS work on transfer pricing under the BEPS Action Plan, there will still be situations where income allocated to a CFC could be subject to CFC rules. For example, current work on transfer pricing may allow a funding return to be allocated to a low-function cash box that just provided financing.[2] If that cash box were a low-tax foreign subsidiary and a country were to choose to subject that return to CFC taxation, this choice would be consistent with the BEPS Action Plan. CFC rules can also be used after the application of transfer pricing rules to address situations where the transfer pricing rules were implemented or applied in a way that is inconsistent with the goals of the *Action Plan on Base Erosion and Profit Shifting* (BEPS Action Plan, OECD, 2013).[3]

1.1.3 Effectively preventing avoidance while reducing administrative and compliance burdens

10. A third policy consideration is how to achieve effective rules that do not unduly increase compliance costs and administrative burdens. Although one of the benefits of CFC rules can be their relatively mechanical application, CFC rules that are entirely mechanical may not be as effective as rules that allow more flexibility.[4] However, flexibility can also create uncertainty, which may affect the costs of both applying and complying with CFC rules. CFC rules must strike a balance between the reduced complexity inherent in mechanical rules and the effectiveness of more subjective rules. This policy consideration is reflected most clearly in rules on defining income. In that context, although an approach that attributes income based purely on its formal classification may reduce administrative and compliance burdens, such an approach may be less effective, and countries with existing CFC rules have generally opted to combine

this approach with less mechanical substance analyses to ensure that the income that is attributed in fact arises from base erosion and profit shifting. Concerns about the administrative burden of substance-based rules can, however, be reduced by including suitably targeted CFC exemptions such as an exemption for companies that are not subject to a lower rate of tax.

1.1.4 Avoiding double taxation

11. An additional consideration is how to avoid double taxation. As CFC rules effectively subject the income of a foreign subsidiary to taxation in the parent jurisdiction, they can lead to double taxation if, for example, the subsidiary is also subject to taxation in the CFC jurisdiction. Double taxation concerns can be limited by incorporating tax rate exemptions, which are discussed in the next section, into CFC rules. Existing CFC rules also seek to prevent double taxation through provisions such as foreign tax credits. These provisions are outlined in the discussion of the sixth building block in Chapter 7.

1.2 Specific policy objectives

12. Whilst the above policy objectives are consistent among most jurisdictions with CFC rules, individual jurisdictions may design CFC rules to achieve a variety of other policy objectives. This is inevitable given that CFC rules are part of a jurisdiction's general system of taxation and the underlying systems vary. As a result, CFC rules also vary significantly in how they prioritise different policy objectives. Two fundamental differences that can affect the design of CFC rules are (i) whether a jurisdiction has a worldwide tax system or a territorial tax system and (ii) whether a jurisdiction is a Member State of the European Union.

1.2.1 Worldwide and territorial systems

13. If a jurisdiction has a worldwide tax system, its CFC rules could apply broadly to any income that is not being currently taxed in the parent jurisdiction and still remain consistent with the parent jurisdiction's overall tax system. If, however, a jurisdiction has a territorial tax system, it may be more consistent for its CFC rules to apply narrowly and only subject income that should have been taxed in the parent jurisdiction to CFC taxation. In reality, jurisdictions' tax systems are almost never purely worldwide nor purely territorial but fall within a spectrum between these two. This may influence the policy choices that jurisdictions make in terms of how they address international competitiveness and how they address base stripping.

1.2.1.1 Striking a balance between taxing foreign income and maintaining competitiveness

14. In designing CFC rules, a balance must be struck between taxing foreign income and the competitiveness concerns inherent in rules that tax the income of foreign subsidiaries. CFC rules raise two primary types of competitiveness concerns. First, jurisdictions with CFC rules that apply broadly may find themselves at a competitive disadvantage relative to jurisdictions without CFC rules (or with narrower CFC rules) because foreign subsidiaries owned by resident companies will be taxed more heavily than locally owned companies in the foreign jurisdiction. This competitive disadvantage may in turn lead to distortions, for instance it may impact on where groups choose to locate their head office or increase the risk of inversions, and it may also impact on

ownership or capital structures where groups attempt to avoid the impact of CFC rules.[5] CFC rules can therefore run the risk of restricting or distorting real economic activity. Second, multinational enterprises resident in countries with robust CFC rules may find themselves at a competitive disadvantage relative to multinational enterprises resident in countries without such rules (or with CFC rules that apply to a significantly lower rate or narrower base). This competitiveness concern arises because the foreign subsidiaries of the first MNEs will be subject to a higher effective tax rate on the income of those subsidiaries than the foreign subsidiaries of the second MNEs due to the application of CFC rules, even when both subsidiaries are operating in the same country.

15. To address these concerns, jurisdictions with territorial systems are more likely to tax only income that was clearly diverted from the parent jurisdiction, thereby prioritising competitiveness. In contrast, jurisdictions with worldwide systems are more likely to tax more income under CFC rules, thereby prioritising taxation of foreign income. Because existing tax systems are almost never pure worldwide systems nor pure territorial systems, CFC rules typically exempt so-called "active" income that is, or is more likely to be, linked to real economic activity in the foreign subsidiary. This approach may not be entirely effective in combatting BEPS, but, in developing recommendations for the design of CFC rules, the balance between taxing foreign income and maintaining competitiveness needs to be kept in mind.

16. Another way to maintain competitiveness would be to ensure that more countries implement similar CFC rules. This is therefore a space where countries working collectively and adopting similar rules could reduce the competitiveness concerns that individual countries may have when considering whether to implement CFC rules.

1.2.1.2 Preventing base stripping

17. Where CFC rules are intended to prevent group companies from shifting income to CFCs, this does not necessarily mean that CFC rules only protect the base of the parent jurisdiction. CFC rules can either focus only on protecting the parent jurisdiction's base or protect against both stripping of the parent jurisdiction's base and foreign-to-foreign stripping. Rules that focus on stripping of the parent jurisdiction define CFC income to include only that income that has been diverted or shifted from the parent jurisdiction, while those that focus on foreign-to-foreign stripping include any income that could have been earned in any jurisdiction other than the CFC jurisdiction. Under the first type of rule, which focuses on stripping of the parent jurisdiction's base, income of the CFC that was separated from activities that took place in a third country would not be subject to CFC taxation. Under the second type of rule, which also includes foreign-to-foreign stripping, this same income would be subject to CFC taxation.[6]

18. CFC rules that focus only on parent jurisdiction stripping may not be as effective against BEPS arrangements for two reasons. First, it may not be possible to determine which country's base has been stripped (for example, in the case of stateless income). Second, even if it were possible to determine which country's base was stripped, the BEPS Action Plan aims to prevent erosion of all tax bases, including those of third countries. This issue may be of particular relevance for developing countries because there may be more of an incentive to structure through low-tax jurisdictions in the absence of CFC rules that focus on foreign-to-foreign stripping.[7]

1.2.2 CFC rules within the European Union

19. A particular competitiveness concern may arise in the context of the European Union. Since 2006,[8] it is generally acknowledged that the European Court of Justice's (ECJ) case law imposes limitations on CFC rules that apply within the European Union. Therefore, whilst recommendations developed under this Action Item need to be broad enough to be effective in combatting BEPS they also need to be adaptable, where necessary, to enable EU members to comply with EU law. This policy consideration affects all jurisdictions, including those that are not Member States of the European Union, because recommendations that are inconsistent with EU law would mean that Member States could not adopt those recommendations to apply within the European Union. This in turn would mean that multinational groups that are based in jurisdictions that are not EU Member States could be at a competitive disadvantage compared to multinational groups that are based in Member States since the latter groups would not be subject to equally robust CFC rules.

20. In *Cadbury Schweppes*[9] and subsequent cases, the ECJ has stated that CFC rules and other tax provisions that apply to cross-border transactions and that are justified by the prevention of tax avoidance must "specifically target wholly artificial arrangements which do not reflect economic reality and whose only purpose would be to obtain a tax advantage".[10] The ECJ's jurisprudence applies to all Member States of the European Union and the European Economic area (EEA),[11] and it applies when the parent jurisdiction and the CFC jurisdiction are both within the EEA.

21. The aim of this report is to set out recommendations for effective CFC rules that can be implemented in all jurisdictions. Where recommendations are made, they are the same for EU Member States and non-EU Member States. However, where there are options, EU Member States will need to ensure that they make choices that are consistent with EU law.[12]

22. Although the determination of how to comply with EU treaty freedoms is the decision of each individual EU Member State, in designing CFC rules, EU Member States could potentially consider the following when implementing adaptable and durable CFC rules:

- Including a substance analysis that would only subject taxpayers to CFC rules if the CFCs did not engage in genuine economic activities. Some Member States have already modified their CFC rules so that they do not apply to genuine economic activities and are therefore consistent with their understanding of the ECJ's "wholly artificial arrangements" limitation.
- Applying CFC rules equally to both domestic subsidiaries and cross-border subsidiaries. A CFC rule will only be found inconsistent with the freedom of establishment if the rule itself discriminates against non-residents. This was made clear in Cadbury Schweppes, where the ECJ focused on the difference in treatment under UK CFC rules between a UK controlled company and a non-resident controlled company. The Court explained this focus by stating:

That difference in treatment creates a tax disadvantage for the resident company to which the legislation on CFCs is applicable. Even taking into account [...] the fact referred to by the national court that such a resident company does not pay, on the profits of a CFC within the scope of application of that legislation, more tax than that which would have been payable on those profits if they had been

> *made by a subsidiary established in the United Kingdom, the fact remains that under such legislation the resident company is taxed on profits of another legal person. That is not the case for a resident company with a subsidiary taxed in the United Kingdom or a subsidiary established outside that Member State which is not subject to a lower level of taxation.*[13]

Therefore, if a CFC rule treats domestic subsidiaries the same as cross-border subsidiaries, it arguably should not be treated as discriminatory under the case law of the ECJ, and no justification is needed. Such an approach would attribute the allocable income of any controlled company, whether foreign or domestic, to its resident shareholders.[14]

- Applying CFC rules to transactions that are "partly wholly artificial". Even if a direct tax rule in a EU Member State is found to implicate the freedom of establishment and to discriminate, it may still be upheld if it is justified and proportionate. Although earlier CFC cases found CFC rules in EU Member States to be justified and proportionate only if they were limited to wholly artificial arrangements, two more recent developments in the ECJ's analysis suggest that CFC rules may now be justified and proportionate even if they apply beyond wholly artificial arrangements. The first development is that cases have suggested that rules may be justified by the need to prevent tax avoidance if they are targeted at arrangements that are not wholly artificial. In Thin Cap Group Litigation, for example, the ECJ stated that, in determining whether thin cap legislation was justified by the need to prevent abusive practices, the Court should determine "whether the transaction in question represents, in whole or in part, a purely artificial arrangement, the essential purpose of which is to circumvent the tax legislation of that Member State".[15] This wording suggests that a CFC rule in a EU Member State that targets income earned by a CFC that is not itself wholly artificial may be justified so long as the transaction giving rise to the income is at least partly artificial.

- Designing CFC rules to explicitly ensure a balanced allocation of taxing power. The ECJ has suggested that Member State tax provisions may not be restricted to wholly artificial arrangements if they are justified by a reason other than the need to prevent tax avoidance. In both SGI[16] and Oy AA,[17] for example, the ECJ stated that the rules in question could be justified notwithstanding the fact that they were not restricted to wholly artificial arrangements because they were justified by the need to maintain a balanced allocation of taxing rights. In SGI, the ECJ clarified that this "justification may be accepted, in particular, where the system in question is designed to prevent conduct capable of jeopardising the right of a Member State to exercise its tax jurisdiction in relation to activities carried out in its territory".[18] Although the Court has not yet found that CFC rules are justified by the need to maintain a balanced allocation of taxing rights, these cases suggest that CFC rules could be permitted to apply more broadly if they could be explained by the need for a Member State to tax profits arising from activities carried out in its territory.

Notes

1. See, e.g., Fleming, J. Clifton Jr., Peroni, Robert J. and Shay, Stephen E., *Worse than Exemption*, 59 Emory L.J. 79 (2009).

2. See the 2015 Report on Action 8-10: *Aligning Transfer Pricing Outcomes With Value Creation* (OECD, 2015) which allocates a risk-free financial return to an entity that lacks the ability to control risks.

3. CFC rules also interact with rules other than transfer pricing rules. In the 2014 Deliverable on *Neutralising the Effects of Hybrid Mismatch Arrangements* (OECD, 2014), for example, Recommendation 5 recognised the importance of CFC rules when it encouraged jurisdictions to improve their CFC rules to prevent deduction/no-inclusion outcomes arising in respect of payments to a reverse hybrid.

4. Entirely mechanical CFC rules also may not be compatible with EU law for the reasons set out later in this chapter.

5. There is a perception that robust CFC rules can lead to inversions, that is, that groups will change the residence of the parent company to escape the effect of CFC rules. However, whilst it is likely that CFC rules will increase the risk of inversions, they will not be the only factor and other issues such as tax rate and the general system of taxation (e.g., worldwide or territorial) will also play a role. For this reason inversions, and the rules that some countries have adopted to combat them, are not covered in this report, but countries may want to consider them as a separate matter.

6. Rules that allow companies to elect whether their subsidiaries are treated as partnerships or corporations also narrow the focus of CFC rules, with the result that they do not prevent foreign-to-foreign stripping. The modified hybrid mismatch rule discussed in Chapter 2, however, is designed to eliminate the effect of such an election for CFC rules and may therefore reduce the availability of this option.

7. For more on the effect of Action Item 3 and the other action items on developing countries, see the BEPS Action Plan and the BEPS Report, both of which refer to the knock-on effect of CFC rules on source countries.

8. In 2006, the European Court of Justice issued its opinion in Cadbury Schweppes plc and Cadbury Schweppes Overseas Ltd v. Commissioners of Inland Revenue, C-196/04. This case considered the compatibility of Member State CFC rules with the EU treaty freedoms.

9. Cadbury Schweppes plc and Cadbury Schweppes Overseas Ltd v. Commissioners of Inland Revenue, C-196/04. More recent cases have echoed the decision in Cadbury Schweppes. In Itelcar – Automóveis de Aluguer Lda. v. Fazenda Pública, Case C-282/12 (3 October 2013), the ECJ made it clear that a national measure restricting the fundamental EU freedoms may be justified where it specifically targets wholly artificial arrangements which do not reflect economic reality and the sole purpose of which is to avoid the tax normally payable on the profits generated by activities carried out on the national territory. In Itelcar the ECJ went on to say that it is apparent from the case-law of the Court that, where rules are predicated on an assessment of objective and verifiable elements for the purposes of determining

whether a transaction represents a wholly artificial arrangement entered into for tax reasons alone, they may be regarded as not going beyond what is necessary to prevent tax evasion and avoidance, if, on each occasion on which the existence of such an arrangement cannot be ruled out, those rules give the taxpayer an opportunity, without subjecting him to undue administrative constraints, to provide evidence of any commercial justification that there may have been for that transaction.

10. Haribo Lakritzen Hans Riegel BetriebsgmbH and Österreichische Salinen AG v. Finanzamt Linz, Joined Cases C-436/08 and C-437/08, paragraph 165.

11. The ECJ's jurisprudence applies to countries that are not Member States of the European Union to the extent that it interprets the fundamental freedoms protected by the Agreement on the European Economic Area.

12. Countries that are not Member States of the European Union could also implement the modifications adopted by EU Member States.

13. Cadbury Schweppes, paragraph 45.

14. At least one jurisdiction already applies such an approach. Denmark's legislation has the effect that there is no different treatment, no matter whether the parent company owns a subsidiary resident in Denmark, a foreign subsidiary resident in the EU/EEA or a foreign subsidiary resident outside the EU/EEA.

15. Test Claimants in the Thin Cap Group Litigation v. Commissioners of Inland Revenue, C-524/04, paragraph 81 (emphasis added).

16. Société de Gestion Industrielle (SGI) v. Belgian State, C-311/08 (21 January 2010) (holding that the freedom of establishment did not prevent Member States from requiring profit adjustments in the case of non-arm's length transactions involving non-resident parties).

17. Oy AA, C-231/05 (18 July 2007) (holding that the freedom of establishment did not prevent Member States from limiting interest deductions for intra-group transfers to payments made to resident companies).

18. SGI, paragraph 60.

Bibliography

Fleming J. Clifton Jr, Peroni Robert J. and Shay Stephen E. (2009), *Worse than Exemption*, 59 Emory L.J. 79 (2009).

OECD (2015), *Aligning Transfer Pricing Outcomes with Value Creation, Actions 8-10 - 2015 Final Reports*, OECD/G20 Base Erosion and Profit Shifting Project, OECD Publishing, Paris, http://dx.doi.org/10.1787/9789264241244-en.

OECD (2014), *Neutralising the Effects of Hybrid Mismatch Arrangements*, OECD Publishing, Paris, http://dx.doi.org/10.1787/9789264218819-en.

OECD (2013), *Action Plan on Base Erosion and Profit Shifting*, OECD Publishing, Paris, http://dx.doi.org/10.1787/9789264202719-en.

Chapter 2

Rules for defining a CFC

23. In order to establish whether CFC rules apply, a jurisdiction must consider two questions: (i) whether a foreign entity is of the type that would be considered a CFC and (ii) whether the parent company has sufficient influence or control over the foreign entity for the foreign entity to be a CFC.

2.1 Recommendations

24. In the context of whether an entity is of the type that would be considered a CFC, the recommendation is to broadly define entities that are within scope so that, in addition to including corporate entities, CFC rules could also apply to certain transparent entities and permanent establishments (PEs) if those entities earn income that raises BEPS concerns and those concerns are not addressed in another way. A further recommendation is to include a form of hybrid mismatch rule to prevent entities from circumventing CFC rules through different tax treatment in different jurisdictions.

25. In the context of control, the recommendation is that CFC rules should at least apply both a legal and an economic control test so that satisfaction of either test results in control. Countries may also include de facto tests to ensure that legal and economic control tests are not circumvented. A CFC should be treated as controlled where residents (including corporate entities, individuals, or others) hold, at a minimum, more than 50% control, although countries that want to achieve broader policy goals or prevent circumvention of CFC rules may set their control threshold at a lower level. This level of control could be established through the aggregated interest of related parties or unrelated resident parties or from aggregating the interests of any taxpayers that are found to be acting in concert. Additionally, CFC rules should apply where there is either direct or indirect control.

2.2 Explanation

2.2.1 Entity considerations

26. Although CFC rules would appear based on their name only to apply to corporate entities, many countries include trusts, partnerships and PEs in limited circumstances to ensure that companies in the parent jurisdiction cannot circumvent CFC rules just by changing the legal form of their subsidiaries.

27. Transparent entities such as partnerships should not be treated as CFCs to the extent that their income is already taxed in the parent jurisdiction on a current basis. However, if a transparent entity earns income that raises BEPS concerns and that is not

taxed in the parent jurisdiction, CFC rules could apply in one of two ways. First, CFC rules could treat the transparent entity as a CFC to ensure that CFC income did not escape CFC taxation due to different entity treatment in the CFC jurisdiction. This situation could arise if, for example, an entity that was a taxable entity under the laws of the parent jurisdiction was a partnership under the laws of the CFC jurisdiction. Second, CFC rules could subject the income of a transparent entity that was owned by a CFC to tax as income of the CFC to ensure that the CFC could not shift income to the transparent entity in order to avoid CFC rules.

28. PEs may need to be subject to CFC rules in two circumstances. First, CFC rules should be broad enough to potentially apply to a situation where a foreign entity has a PE in another country. Second, where a parent jurisdiction exempts the income of a PE[1], the income of that PE could potentially raise the same concerns as income arising in a foreign subsidiary. Where this is the case, the parent jurisdiction could address this either by denying the exemption or by applying CFC rules to the PE.

29. A further issue that arises in determining which entities could be CFCs is how to treat hybrid tax planning in situations where the parent jurisdiction's rules concerning characterisation of instruments and entities results in payments that might otherwise be attributed under CFC rules being ignored or treated as being outside the scope of CFC rules. For example, entity classification rules in the parent jurisdiction can allow the payer and payee in a multinational group to be treated as the same entity for CFC purposes so that a deductible intra-group payment between these entities is not taken into account under the parent's CFC rules. These rules ultimately exclude income that would otherwise be attributable as CFC income and they have this effect because they do not recognise certain entities. To the extent that the payment is deductible in the payer's jurisdiction this gives rise to foreign to foreign base erosion issues.

30. It is recommended that countries address this issue. One way to do so could be to consider a modified hybrid mismatch rule that requires an intragroup payment to a CFC to be taken into account in calculating the parent company's CFC income.[2] A possible approach would take an intragroup payment into account if:

- The payment is not included in CFC income.
- The payment would have been included in CFC income if the parent jurisdiction had classified the entities and arrangements in the same way as the payer or payee jurisdiction.

31. The example below explains how this rule might operate. In the structure illustrated below, A Co, a company resident in Country A, holds all the shares of B Co, a company resident in Country B. B Co, in turn, holds all the shares in C Co, a company resident in Country C. Country A and Country C are high tax jurisdictions while Country B is a low tax jurisdiction. C Co is a disregarded entity for Country A tax purposes. C Co borrows money from B Co, and because C Co is treated as transparent under the laws of Country A, the payment of interest to B Co is ignored under the laws of Country A and therefore not included within the calculation of CFC income for Country A purposes. Note that this example would not currently be caught by the rules recommended under Action Item 2 as this payment does not create a hybrid mismatch under the rules of either Country B or Country C, which are the residence jurisdictions of the counterparties. Instead, it only creates a hybrid mismatch under the laws of Country A, which is the country that treats C Co as transparent.

Figure 2.1 Modified hybrid mismatch rule

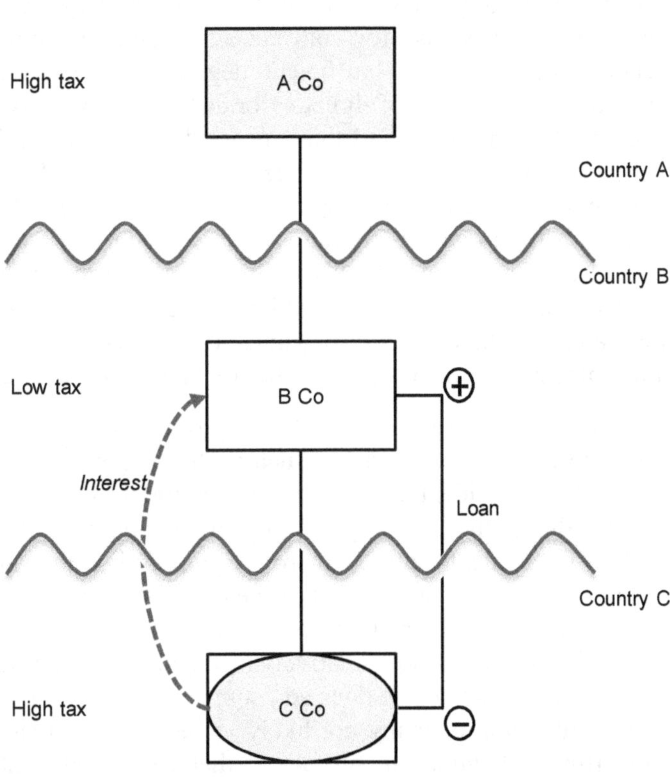

32. The interest payment is a deductible intra-group payment. The reason it is not included in the calculation of CFC income is due to the treatment of the payer under the laws of the parent jurisdiction. Under the rule set out above, the payment would be included as an item of interest paid by another CFC when calculating A Co's CFC income.

33. While the example illustrated above involves a conflict in entity classification, a similar result can be achieved using a loan that is treated as equity for Country A purposes (so that the interest payment is characterised under Country A's CFC rules as an exempt dividend). The effect can also be achieved by exploiting differences in the treatment of residence for tax purposes. For example, Country A, applying its own rules on tax residency, could treat B Co as tax resident in Country C so that the interest payment is ignored under a same country exception,[3] under which Country A's CFC rules do not include income in CFC income if it was received from taxpayers resident in the CFC jurisdiction. As these arrangements all rely on a conflict in the characterisation of the entity or instrument they would also be caught under the rule outlined above.

2.2.2 Control

34. The definition of control requires two different determinations: (i) the type of control that is required and (ii) the level of that control.

2.2.2.1 Type of control

35. Control can be established in various ways, which are outlined below.

- ***Legal control*** generally looks at a resident's holding of share capital to determine the percentage of voting rights held in a subsidiary. Legal control is a relatively mechanical test that is easy for both tax administrations and taxpayers to apply and reflects the fact that a sufficient degree of voting rights should enable residents to elect the board of directors or an equivalent body responsible for the affairs of the foreign entity and thus ensure that a CFC acts in accordance with their instructions. However, corporate law often provides a large degree of flexibility in designing the share structure of a corporation, thus enabling the use of artificial share terms and structures to circumvent the control requirement. A focus on legal control is therefore likely to be too narrow, and most countries also use a concept of economic control. Although tests that consider the entitlement to acquire shares, and therefore voting rights, through certain contingent rights such as options may help mitigate some of the weaknesses of legal control.

- ***Economic control*** focuses on rights to the profits, as well as capital and assets of a company in certain circumstances such as dissolution or liquidation. Such a test recognises that a resident can control an entity through an entitlement to the underlying value of the company even where they do not hold the majority of the shares. This entitlement may result from rights to the proceeds in the event of a disposal of the entity's share capital or the entity's assets on a winding up. It may also include rights to a distribution of profits other than on a disposal or winding up. Economic control is also a relatively mechanical test that focuses on facts that can be objectively assessed. It does add some complexity but in reality those with a majority stake in a company are likely to be aware of that fact and may have other reporting obligations in respect of that controlled relationship. However, economic control rules may be circumvented, most obviously by means of group reorganisations involving the insertion of a new group holding company. In such situations, both legal and economic control may change even though there is little or no change in the underlying business or the level of decision-making and business control exercised by the previous parent.

- ***De facto control*** can look at similar factors to those considered by many countries when considering where a company is resident for tax purposes. For instance, countries can look at who takes the top-level decisions regarding the affairs of the foreign company or who has the ability to direct or influence its day-to-day activities. Another approach could focus on any particular contractual ties with the CFC that permit taxpayers to exert a dominant influence over it. However, a de facto control test generally operates as an anti-avoidance rule to ensure that other control tests are not circumvented. De facto control tests therefore require a significant analysis of the facts and circumstances and some subjective assessment of these. If applied in all cases, this will lead to added costs, complexity and uncertainty for taxpayers. In addition, based on countries' experience in operating residence rules, the type of criteria mentioned above may also be relatively easy to avoid and therefore difficult for a tax administration to prove.

- ***Control based on consolidation*** can look at whether a non-resident company is consolidated in the accounts of a resident company based on accounting principles (e.g. International Financial Reporting Standards, or IFRS). This is not fundamentally different from the approaches mentioned above. In fact, like the legal and de facto control tests, accounting principles also refer to criteria such as voting rights or other rights to exercise a dominant influence over another entity, but they use these criteria to establish whether or not an entity should be consolidated. For example, under IFRS 10 a taxpayer should consolidate any entity if, for instance, it has rights that give the power to direct the activities that most significantly affect the subsidiary's returns. The power may be based on voting rights in relevant areas of the subsidiary's business activity or generally on a controlling influence over the subsidiary which effectively tests legal and de facto control.

36. The above approaches are often combined to prevent circumvention and to ensure that rules operate effectively. Based on the above analysis, a control test should focus on a combined approach that includes at least legal and economic control. Both of these tests are reasonably mechanical and so should limit the administrative and compliance burden involved. However, countries could also consider supplementing these tests with either a de facto test or a test based on consolidation for accounting purposes. Both of these, but particularly a broad de facto test, could increase complexity and compliance costs. Therefore countries that are attracted to using one of the latter two tests to address specific problems (such as those raised by inversions) may find that these problems could be better addressed with separate targeted provisions rather than through an extension of the concept of control for CFC purposes.

2.2.2.2 Level of control

37. Once a CFC regime has established what actually confers control, the next question is how much control is enough for the CFC rules to apply. If the aim is to catch all situations where the controlling party has the ability to shift profits to a foreign company, then, as a minimum, CFC rules would need to capture situations where resident taxpayers have a legal or economic interest in the foreign entity of more than 50%. Some existing rules find control when the parent owns exactly 50%, but the majority of rules require more than 50% control. Because owning 50% or less could still allow parent companies to exert influence in certain situations, jurisdictions are free to lower their control threshold below 50%.[4]

38. The determination of whether this 50% threshold has been met is straightforward when control is held by a single resident shareholder. Shareholders can exert influence in other situations, however, and existing rules generally attempt to capture these instances as well with their control rules. The general principle underlying control tests is that minority shareholders that are acting together to exert influence should have their interests aggregated when determining whether the control test has been met. Whether or not minority shareholders are acting together can be determined in at least three ways, and it is recommended that jurisdictions adopt one of these approaches to ensure that minority shareholders who are in fact exerting influence are taken into account when determining whether there is control.

39. The first way of determining whether minority shareholders are acting together is to apply an "acting-in-concert" test, which applies a fact-based analysis to determine whether the shareholders are in fact acting together to influence the CFC. If they are, their interests will be aggregated to determine whether the CFC is subject to CFC rules. This approach is not very common because it creates significant administrative and compliance burdens, but one of its advantages is that it may more accurately identify when shareholders are in fact acting together than a more mechanical test. An example of how an acting-in-concert test would work is illustrated below.

Figure 2.2 Control interest held by unrelated parties acting in concert

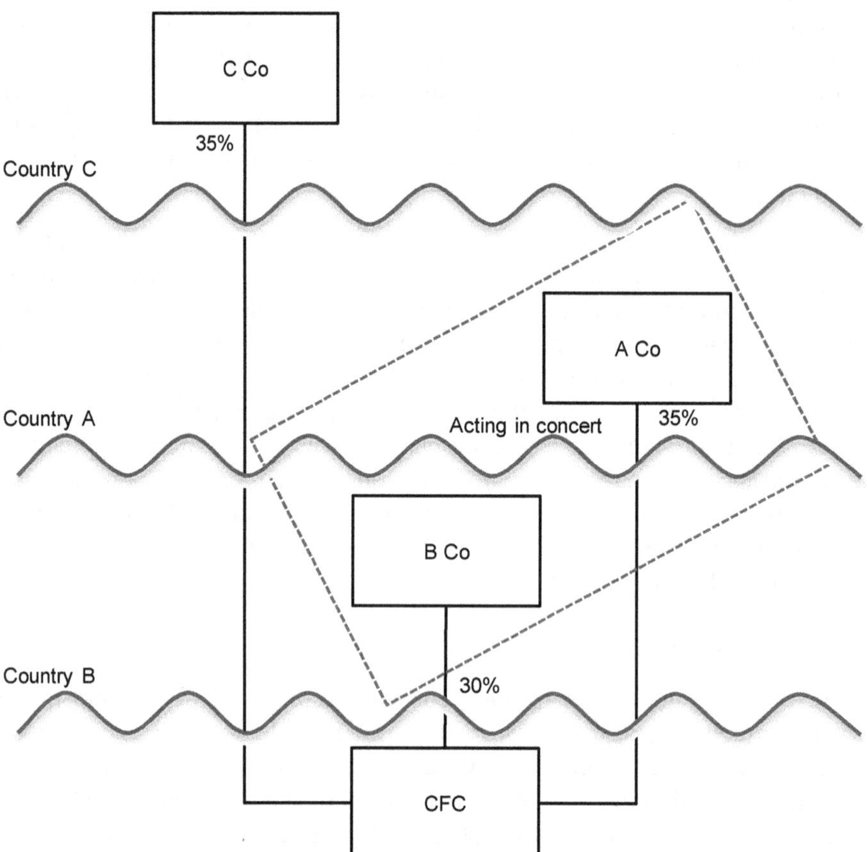

40. C Co, A Co and B Co are all unrelated parties. Country A's CFC rules require a controlling interest of more than 50% before they can be applied. There is no other resident taxpayer in Country A so unless Country A has an acting-in-concert rule that aggregates the interest of both residents and non-residents, and the acting in concert rule can be shown to apply, then there will be no attribution of the income of CFC to A Co. As mentioned above, an acting-in-concert rule would add complexity and compliance costs, especially where it is applied to both residents and non-residents. However, it could also prevent circumvention of CFC rules.[5]

41. The second way that some rules determine whether minority shareholders are acting together is to look to the relationship of the parties. If rules only include the interests of *related* parties when determining whether the 50% threshold has been met, this would eliminate the need for a fact-based acting-in-concert test, but it will apply more narrowly since it focuses more directly on the profit shifting opportunities created by structures involving related parties. However, since BEPS structures often involve wholly owned subsidiaries or at least subsidiaries owned by related parties, a focus on related parties may still capture most structures that raise BEPS concerns.[6] An example of how a related party test would work is illustrated below.

Figure 2.3 Control interest held by related parties

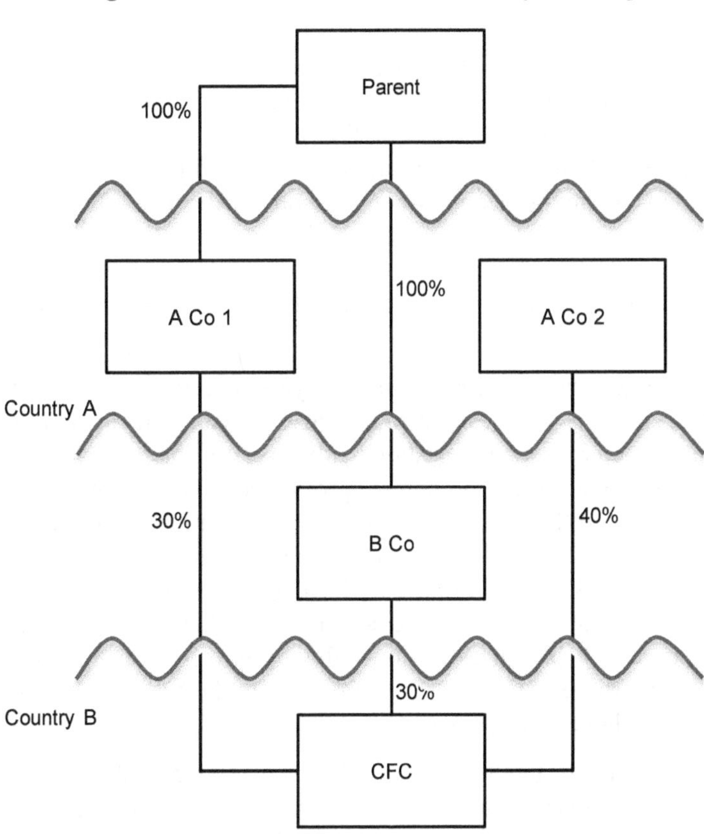

42. A Co 1 and A Co 2 are unrelated residents in Country A. For Country A's CFC rules to apply, related parties or residents that act in concert must hold an aggregate interest in the CFC of more than 50%. Parent Co splits the interest in CFC between A Co 1 and B Co, in order to circumvent the control requirement in country A. If, however, Country A applied a related party rule that aggregates the interests of related parties to determine control, then A Co 1 would be found to be a controlling shareholder because of the shared ownership between A Co 1 and B Co, which are both owned by Parent. This would mean that 30% of the income of CFC would be attributed to A Co 1. No income would be attributed to A Co 2. The same outcome is likely to arise under an acting-in-concert test. Whether or not income is attributed to B Co would depend on the rules in operation in Country B but if they operated the same form of related party rule, then 30% of the income of CFC would also be attributed to B Co.

43. The third way that CFC rules determine whether minority shareholders are exerting influence over the CFC is to impose a concentrated ownership requirement. In the United States, for example, the interests, of all residents, in the CFC are aggregated so long as each interest is higher than 10%. This approach leads to the interests of a concentrated group of residents being considered, and it also eliminates the need for separate rules for attribution, since the 10% threshold for control can also be used to determine which residents will have income allocated to them. Alternatively, a concentrated ownership requirement could require that ownership be divided between a small number of resident shareholders (e.g. 5 or fewer), regardless of their ownership percentage, but this may raise administrative and compliance concerns. CFC rules that aggregate all interests above a low threshold (e.g. 10%), or that focus just on the number

of owners, may not always accurately identify whether taxpayers are in reality acting together.

44. A concentrated ownership rule can be illustrated with reference to Figure 2.3 above. If Country A expanded its control requirement and applied its rules where there were a small group of resident shareholders, in this situation A Co 1 and A Co 2, then the CFC rules would apply and 30% of the income of CFC would be attributed to A Co 1 and 40% to A Co 2. This would prevent circumvention of the rules but would attribute income to A Co 2. This might not be a concern in the context of a 40% holding but a test that focuses on a small group of residents would potentially attribute profits to A Co 2 even if it was not acting in concert with A Co 1 and had no real ability to transfer income or profits to the CFC.

45. Including the interests of non-resident taxpayers in any of these three approaches could add to the complexity of the control provisions but such an addition could be considered if countries were concerned about either related or unrelated parties acting together to try and circumvent the CFC control provisions.[7] The recommendations above therefore do not recommend that non-residents are also taken into account in determining the level of control, but, as with all recommendations, the recommendation included in this document only establishes a minimum, and jurisdictions with different policy aims could include non-resident interests when determining whether the 50% threshold (or any lower threshold) was met. If jurisdictions chose this option, limiting taxation of resident taxpayers to their actual share of CFC income (rather than the aggregated amount) should eliminate any concerns about double taxation.

46. Regardless of which of the three approaches is taken, control should be defined to include both direct and indirect control as profit-shifting opportunities also arise where a subsidiary is held indirectly through an intermediate holding company. If CFC rules do not apply to indirect holdings then they can be very easily sidestepped. The example below illustrates one of the questions raised by indirect control, which is whether a level of indirect control that falls below the control threshold should still lead to a finding of control if the control threshold is met at each level in the chain of ownership.

Figure 2.4 Calculation of indirect control interest

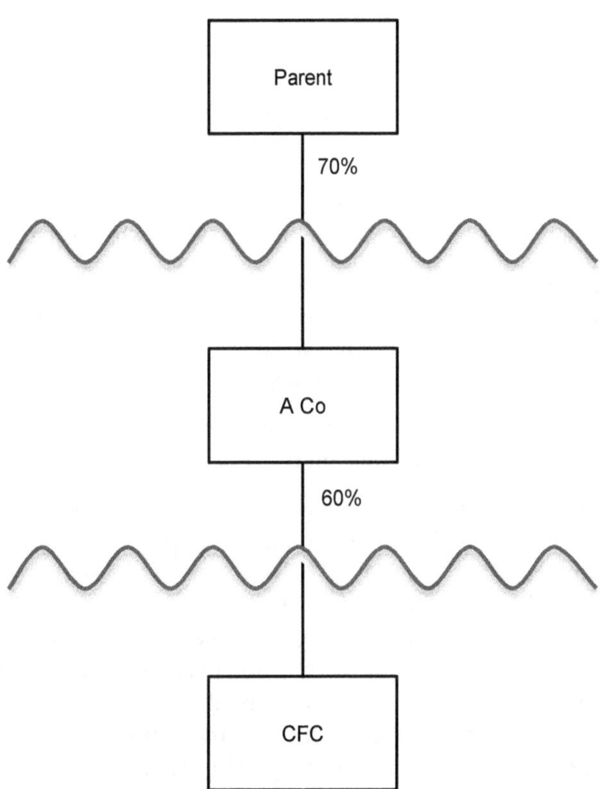

47. In this example, Parent has a 70% interest in A Co, which holds a 60% interest in CFC. There is therefore more than 50% control at each tier, but Parent itself only has an interest of 42% (70% x 60%) of CFC. Despite this limited legal control, A Co has enough economic control to influence CFC and Parent has enough economic control to influence A Co, so it is recommended that CFC rules should find Parent to have sufficient influence over CFC to meet the control threshold since the control threshold is met at each level in the chain of ownership.[8] The amount of income attributed to Parent should, however, be limited to its actual economic interest of 42%.

48. Although including both direct and indirect control in the control analysis could arguably increase the potential for double taxation if all countries were to introduce CFC rules, this situation should be addressed with rules to reduce or eliminate double taxation.[9]

49. Determining whether a company in the parent jurisdiction has control also requires a rule determining when control should be established as well as what types of entities can be considered to have control. On the first question, many rules determine control based on how much of an economic or legal interest was held at the end of the year, but jurisdictions concerned about circumvention of this rule can also include anti-abuse provisions or a test that looks at whether the parent company had the necessary level of control at any point during the year. On the second question, in order to ensure that all situations where resident shareholders have the opportunity to shift income into a foreign subsidiary are captured, CFC rules should consider the interests held by all resident taxpayers, rather than limiting this inquiry to corporate entities or other limited groups.

Notes

1. This includes a branch as defined under domestic law that equates to a PE.

2. This is not the only way to tackle this issue. A jurisdiction that implements an excess profits approach similar to that described in Chapter 4, for example, may not need an additional rule to address these types of hybrid mismatches if such an approach does not ignore the income earned in situations such as those illustrated in Figure 2.1.

3. Several countries including the United States have exceptions in their CFC rules for payments made between companies in the same country.

4. Some CFC rules recognise that control can be exercised below 50% ownership. For instance, New Zealand's CFC rules find that the control threshold has been met when a New Zealand resident owns 40% or more of the foreign subsidiary. Note that a much lower control threshold may raise EU legal concerns for Member States' CFC rules, even if they do not apply to CFCs in other Member States. This is because, as the control threshold is reduced, CFC rules may implicate not just the freedom of establishment but the free movement of capital, which applies to Member State rules that are discriminatory toward residents of third countries as well as residents of other Member States. This concern would only arise when the threshold is reduced below the level of "significant influence".

5. A similar scenario to that above could arise where there is a joint venture. Some countries have specific rules to deal with joint ventures. Under the UK CFC rules, a UK resident 40% joint venture partner would be treated as having control if there is a non-UK resident that holds at least 40% and no more than 55% of the legal and economic interest in the joint venture. This rule has a similar effect to an acting-in-concert type rule.

6. This may not capture all structures that raise BEPS concerns, however, and other action items have recognised that unrelated parties may act together to achieve a certain outcome. The work on hybrid mismatch arrangements, for example, includes structured arrangements involving unrelated parties.

7. Non-resident taxpayers whose interests could possibly be included could include family members of resident shareholders or board members of domestic parent companies.

8. For example, once control is established at a level, some CFC rules deem the control at that level to be 100% for the purpose of determining the level of indirect control at the next level.

9. See infra Chapter 7.

Bibliography

International Accounting Standards Board (2011), *International Financial Reporting Standards 10: Consolidated Financial Statements,* London, 2011.

Chapter 3

CFC exemptions and threshold requirements

50. CFC exemptions and threshold requirements can be used to limit the scope of CFC rules by excluding entities that are likely to pose little risk of base erosion and profit shifting and instead focusing attention on cases that are higher-risk because they exhibit some characteristic or behaviour that means there is a greater chance of profit shifting. These provisions can therefore both help make CFC rules more targeted and effective and also reduce the overall level of administrative burden by ensuring that certain companies are not affected by the rules, although these companies may still need to satisfy certain reporting requirements to show that they meet any requirements for these provisions.

3.1 Recommendations

51. The recommendation is to include a tax rate exemption that would allow companies that are subject to an effective tax rate that is sufficiently similar to the tax rate applied in the parent jurisdiction not to be subject to CFC taxation. The effect of this tax rate exemption would be to subject all CFCs with an effective tax rate meaningfully below the rate applied in the parent jurisdiction to CFC rules. This exemption could be combined with a list such as a white list.

3.2 Explanation

52. Three different types of CFC exemptions and threshold requirements were considered by the countries involved in this work:

1. A set de minimis amount below which the CFC rules would not apply
2. An anti-avoidance requirement which would focus CFC rules on situations where there was a tax avoidance motive or purpose
3. A tax rate exemption where CFC rules would only apply to CFCs resident in countries with a lower tax rate than the parent company.

3.2.1 De minimis threshold

53. A de minimis threshold could reduce administrative burdens and make CFC rules more targeted and effective by ensuring that certain companies are not subject to the rules.[1] Many countries' rules already include a de minimis threshold under which income that would otherwise be treated as CFC income is not included in the taxable income of the parent company if it falls under a certain ceiling. Generally, countries provide an entity-based exemption where the entity's attributable income is less than either a certain percentage of the CFC's income or a fixed amount of the CFC's income or where the

taxable profits are less than a fixed amount. Some rules also include a separate cap for certain types of profits that present a higher risk of being diverted. The UK rules, for example, use two different thresholds with a much higher de minimis threshold applying to CFCs that can show that they do not earn much income that is likely to be highly mobile.

54. One possible way that de minimis thresholds can be circumvented is through fragmentation, under which companies split their income amongst multiple subsidiaries, each of which falls below the threshold. Countries' current rules often include safeguards to protect against such circumvention. Although this may add some complexity to the rules, countries' experience has shown that these safeguards may not necessarily be inconsistent with the threshold's purpose of reducing administrative and compliance burdens. For example, the de minimis test under the United States rules includes a general anti-abuse rule which looks at the income of two or more controlled foreign corporations in aggregate and treats it as the income of a single corporation if a principal purpose for separately organising, acquiring, or maintaining such multiple corporations is to prevent income from being treated as attributable under the de minimis test. Although such an anti-abuse rule increases the potential administrative burden of the de minimis threshold, this increased burden is counteracted in the US rule with a rebuttable presumption that automatically treats the income of multiple CFCs as that of a single corporation if the CFCs are related persons and carry on a business previously conducted by a single CFC or carry on a business as partners in a related partnership. Under the German rules, the general de minimis test is subject to the condition that the attributable income must not exceed the same amount at the level of the CFC and at the level of the shareholder. This means that even if the attributable income of one CFC does not exceed the threshold, the CFC may still be subject to CFC rules if the same threshold is exceeded by adding all of a taxpayer's shareholdings in several CFCs. Examples of these two different types of anti-fragmentation rules are set out below.

55. In Figure 3.1, A Group rearranges its operations to ensure that profits that previously arose in a single CFC are split between three CFCs in different territories. After the reorganisation, A Co is the sole shareholder of three controlled foreign corporations. CFC1, CFC2 and CFC3 all have the same taxable year, and they are partners in a foreign entity in Country C classified as a partnership (FP). For their current taxable years, each of the CFCs derives part of its attributable income from the foreign partnership and part from other activities undertaken separately.

Figure 3.1 De minimis test

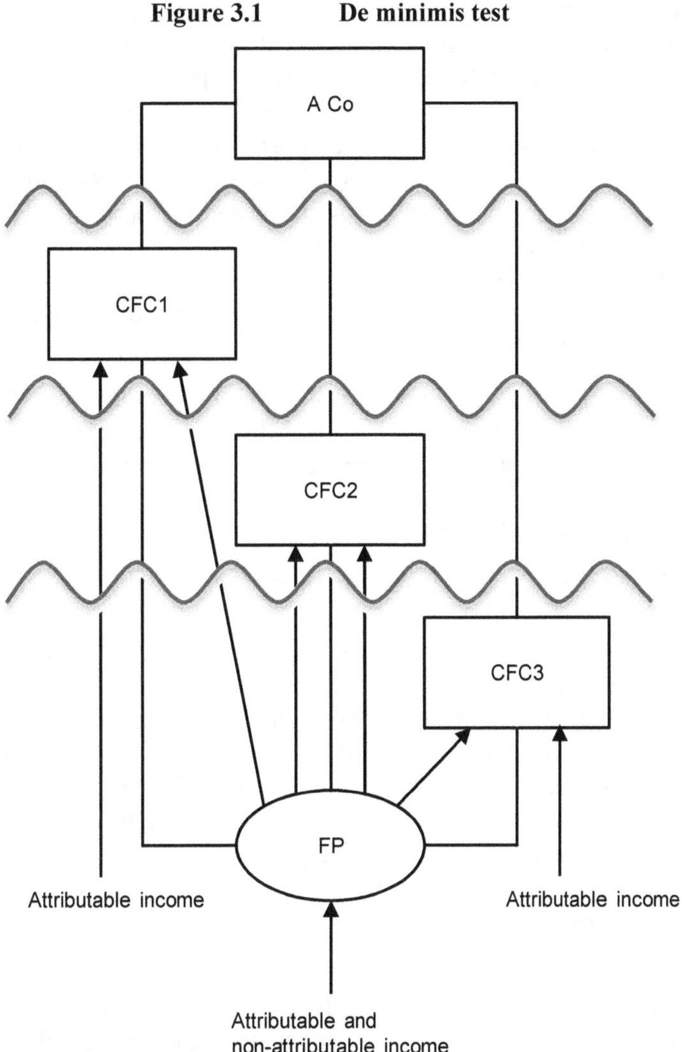

56. Under the de minimis test in Country A, attributable CFC income is not taken into account for the purposes of residence taxation if the sum of the attributable CFC income is less than the lesser of 5% of total income or 1 000 000. Based on the figures in the table below, the attributable income derived by each CFC for its current taxable year, including income derived from the foreign partnership, is less than five percent of the gross income of each CFC or is less than 1 000 000.

	CFC 1	CFC 2	CFC 3
Gross income	3 000 000	7 000 000	11 000 000
5% of gross income	150 000	350 000	550 000
Attributable income	140 000	348 000	547 000

57. Therefore, without the application of an anti-abuse rule, each CFC would be treated as having no attributable income after the application of the de minimis test.

58. If, however, Country A were to have either an anti-abuse rule similar to the US rule or an anti-fragmentation rule similar to the German rule, A Co would be subject to CFC taxation on the income earned by its foreign subsidiaries. If Country A has an anti-

abuse rule that treats the income of all three CFCs as the income of one CFC for the purposes of calculating the de minimis threshold if the CFCs are related persons (or if the principal purpose for separately organising, acquiring, or maintaining such multiple corporations is to prevent income from being treated as attributable under the de minimis test), then the attributable income is aggregated. The sum of the attributable income of the CFCs is 1 035 000, so it exceeds the 1 000 000 de minimis threshold and will be taken into account under Country A's CFC rules. If, instead, Country A has a rule that the attributable income at the level of the shareholder must not exceed the attributable income at the level of the CFC, the de minimis threshold would also be overcome because the attributable income at the level of the shareholder is 1 035 000, while it is significantly less at the level of the CFCs.

59. Therefore, although there is no general recommendation under this building block for or against de minimis thresholds, if jurisdictions choose to implement such a threshold, best practice would be to combine this with an anti-fragmentation rule.

3.2.2 Anti-avoidance requirement

60. An anti-avoidance threshold requirement would only subject transactions and structures that were the result of tax avoidance to CFC rules. This could narrow the effectiveness of CFC rules as preventative measures, and it could also increase the administrative and compliance burdens of CFC rules if it were administrated as an up-front rule. Additionally, an anti-avoidance rule should not be necessary if the rules defining the income within the scope of a CFC regime are properly targeted. An anti-avoidance requirement is therefore not considered further in this report, but this is not intended to imply that an anti-avoidance requirement can never play a role in CFC rules that tackle base erosion and profit shifting.

3.2.3 Tax rate exemption

61. Most CFC rules include a tax rate exemption that exempts CFCs subject to a tax rate above a certain level. Such an exemption is included for two reasons. First, this approach means that the rules only apply to companies that benefit from low foreign taxes and therefore pose the greatest risk of profit shifting. Second, a focus on low-tax CFCs can provide greater certainty for taxpayers and reduce the overall administrative burden. A tax rate exemption can, however, mean that CFC rules do not prevent all base erosion and profit shifting since they still allow erosion of the parent jurisdiction's base to high or medium-tax jurisdictions, so a few jurisdictions do not include such an exemption.

62. There are different ways for jurisdictions to determine when a CFC has paid a low rate of tax. Jurisdictions may require taxpayers to apply a comparative approach on a case-by-case basis, or they may use a black list or white list to simplify the process. Using a list generally eliminates the need for a case-by-case analysis of a CFC's tax rate and is a way of communicating whether jurisdictions apply a lower level of tax. The use of black or white lists can make it easier for tax administrations to determine when CFC rules do and do not apply and for taxpayers to know whether they will be subject to CFC rules, and the use of lists such as a white list is included in the recommendation under this building block. The United Kingdom, for example, has a white list that excludes CFCs located in listed jurisdictions which are sufficiently similar in terms of tax base and tax rate to the United Kingdom, provided that several other conditions are also met.[2] Finland issues a list of tax treaty countries (not including EU Member States) to be considered low-tax based on

nominal tax rates and tax incentives but only regards a company in those countries as a CFC if the company itself pays less than three-fifths of the taxes that would have been paid in Finland. This approach therefore sets a presumption that a CFC is lowly taxed, but that presumption must be supported with an actual comparison of taxes paid. Sweden applies a similar approach under which countries are broken into three categories: (i) countries where no entities would be CFCs; (ii) countries where entities without CFC income would not be CFCs while entities with CFC income would be compared against the tax rate exemption; and (iii) countries where all income will be compared against the tax rate exemption. Australia applies a white list approach under which companies resident in countries with an income tax system comparable to Australia's tax system are not subject to CFC taxation. CFCs in a listed jurisdiction are therefore exempt from Australia's CFC rules unless they are subject to a concessional tax regime.

63. Tax rate exemptions require that the rate at which the CFC was taxed be below a given benchmark. Tax rate exemptions apply one of two benchmarks. They either compare the tax rate in the CFC jurisdiction to a particular fixed rate that is considered low-tax or they compare the tax rate in the CFC jurisdiction to a portion or percentage of the parent country's own rate. Both approaches are equally relevant within the context of designing rules to combat BEPS as both recognise that the incentive to shift profits will be greater where there is a significant differential between effective tax rates.

64. Under the first approach, countries would need to set a fixed tax rate below which their CFC rules would potentially apply. An example of such an approach would be the German CFC rules, which define any level of taxation below 25% as low taxation. The second approach instead calculates the tax rate exemption based on a percentage of the tax that would have been paid to the parent jurisdiction, which thereby includes both tax rate and tax base in the analysis. The UK and Finnish CFC rules provide examples of this approach. Under UK law, there is no low taxation if the "local tax amount" is at least 75% of the "corresponding UK tax". As mentioned above, under the Finnish rules, a low-tax regime is considered to exist if the company itself pays less than three-fifths of the taxes that would have been paid in Finland. Whichever approach is adopted, the benchmark should be meaningfully lower than the tax rate in the country applying the CFC rules. Most CFC rules apply benchmarks that are at the most 75% of the statutory corporate tax rate.

65. Once the benchmark has been set, CFC rules must determine the tax rate in the CFC jurisdiction in order to compare this to the benchmark. Current CFC rules do this in one of two ways. They either compare the benchmark to: (i) the nominal (or statutory) tax rate in the CFC jurisdiction; or (ii) the effective[3] tax rate of the CFC. Although using the statutory tax rate may reduce administrative complexity and compliance costs, the recommendation is to use the effective rate. This latter approach takes into account the tax base or other tax provisions that may increase or reduce the effective rate paid by the CFC and therefore is likely to create a much more accurate comparison than focusing on the statutory tax rate. Using the effective tax rate, however, means that whether the tax rate exemption has been met must be determined in two steps. First, there must be a calculation of the effective tax rate, which requires determining both how much tax the CFC paid and how much income the CFC earned. Second, the effective tax rate must be compared to the benchmark.

66. The determination of the effective tax rate is typically based on the ratio of the actual tax paid in the CFC jurisdiction to the total taxable income either computed according to the rules of the parent/shareholder's country or according to an international accounting standard such as International Financial Reporting Standards (IFRS). This

method generally recognises that even in a situation where the statutory tax rate is not considered a low tax rate, low taxation may occur as a result of (i) reducing the tax base; or (ii) lowering the tax burden by subsequent rebates of taxes paid or through non-enforcement of taxes.[4] This can be illustrated in the following two examples.

a) **Example 1:** A CFC in Country C generates 80 000 of income in one year. Country A applies its CFC rules if the effective tax rate applied to the CFC was below a fixed rate of 25% taking into account the tax base as computed under Country A's rules. Country C allows an exemption of 20% when computing the taxable income to promote investments.

Calculation of actual tax paid in Country C:	
Income in Country C	80 000
Exemption (20%)	16 000
Taxable income	64 000
Corporate tax due (30%)	19 200
Actual tax paid	19 200
Income in Country C:	
Income in Country C5	80 000
Effective tax rate calculation:	
19 200/80 000	24%

b) **Example 2:** A CFC in Country C generates 80 000 of income in one year. Country A applies its CFC rules if the effective tax rate applied to the CFC was below a fixed rate of 25% taking into account the tax base as computed under Country A's rules. Country C does not provide for an exemption to promote investments. However, according to Country C's rules, shareholders of the CFC may claim a refund in the amount of 20% of the corporate income tax paid by the CFC upon distribution of dividends. The dividends would be tax exempt in Country A.

Calculation of actual tax paid in Country C:	
Income	80 000
Taxable income	80 000
Corporate tax due (30%)	24 000
Refund upon distribution (20% of 24 000)	4 800
Actual tax paid	19 200
Income in Country C:	
Income in Country C6	80,000
Effective tax rate calculation:	
19 200/80 000	24%

67. In both Example 1 and Example 2, the tax rate exemption does not apply because the effective tax rate is below the fixed rate of 25%. The calculation of the effective tax rate should therefore ensure that situations such as those illustrated in Example 1 and

Example 2 are subject to CFC rules, and the discussion below provides ways to ensure this.

68. The calculation of the effective tax rate uses a fraction where the numerator is the actual tax paid and the denominator is the CFC's income. Although the determination of the actual tax paid could require proof that tax was in fact collected and not refunded, the definition of the numerator could be more straightforward if it instead focuses just on the final tax burden (including, for example, subsequent rebates of taxes paid and non-enforcement of taxes). The numerator could also include all taxes paid by the CFC that are comparable to the corporate income tax in the parent jurisdiction.

69. Compared to calculating the actual tax paid, the determination of what to include in the total taxable income (i.e., the denominator) may be more problematic. If the denominator were to refer to the foreign tax base, the effective tax rate would equal the statutory tax rate of the CFC jurisdiction,[7] which would undermine the purpose of the effective tax rate calculation. The denominator should therefore be either the tax base in the parent jurisdiction had the CFC income been earned there or the tax base computed according to an international accounting standard such as IFRS, with adjustments made to reflect the tax base reductions that result in low taxation of the CFC income.[8]

70. In theory, the effective tax rate calculation could find a *higher* effective tax rate than the statutory tax rate in the CFC jurisdiction if the base calculated under the rules of the parent jurisdiction is smaller than that calculated under the rules of the CFC jurisdiction. In reality, however, this situation is unlikely to occur much in practice as groups would not structure themselves into jurisdictions where the advantage of a low statutory tax rate is entirely or partially set off by a tax disadvantage in the tax base computation (e.g. non-deductible expenditures).

71. The effective tax rate computation could also be influenced by the "unit" used for the calculation. Country rules generally calculate the effective tax rate on a company-by-company basis, but it could in theory be computed either narrowly or broadly. A narrow approach could, for example, calculate the effective tax rate for each item of income earned by a company. Computing the effective tax rate on a narrower basis allows jurisdictions to apply the tax rate exemption just to the income that has been defined as attributable income under CFC rules. For example, if royalties were subject to taxation under a jurisdiction's definition of CFC income, the tax rate exemption would apply more precisely to that income provided that the effective tax rate was computed narrowly for each type of income. This may also more directly address situations where only certain types of income benefit from a low tax rate, while others are subject to regular taxation. Calculating the effective tax rate on a narrower basis would, however, increase both the administrative complexity and compliance burden associated with the tax rate exemption. A broad approach could calculate the effective tax rate on a company-by-company or country-by-country basis. A country-by-country approach would aggregate the income of all entities of a group in a single country to calculate the effective tax rate. These broader approaches would reduce the administrative complexity and compliance burden compared to the narrow approach, but calculating the tax rate exemption on a country-by-country basis would add complexity compared to doing so on a company-by-company basis because it would require aggregating the calculations for all the CFCs in each jurisdiction rather than just calculating the effective tax rate for each CFC. If CFC jurisdictions exempt Permanent Establishments (PEs) from taxation, the effective tax rate of permanent establishments of a CFC should be calculated separately

from that of the CFC to ensure that the tax rates of the PE and CFC cannot be blended to inappropriately exempt income of a CFC.

Notes

1. A de minimis threshold could also eliminate the need for a special rule for exempting working capital under a transactional approach. See infra Chapter 4.

2. These conditions are that there cannot be more than insignificant amounts of certain defined types of income that are not effectively taxed in the CFC's territory of residence, that none of the CFC's income has been generated using IP that has been effectively transferred from a UK related party in the previous six years, and that the CFC is not involved in any arrangement intended to create a UK tax advantage for any person.

3. The effective tax rate may be computed as an average of the effective tax rates over several years.

4. However, where jurisdictions do not apply a substance analysis as discussed in Chapter 4 they may choose to adjust the calculation of the effective tax rate so that situations where a lower tax burden is justified under commonly agreed standards such as the nexus approach agreed under Action 5 are not considered to affect the effective tax rate calculation for the purposes of applying a CFC regime.

5. The income is calculated according to Country A's rules. All other calculations in this table are calculated using Country C's rules since they were used to determine the tax actually paid to Country C.

6. The income is calculated according to Country A's rules. All other calculations in this table are calculated using Country C's rules since they were used to determine the tax actually paid to Country C.

7. This is, of course, only true if there are no rebates and the tax was in fact collected and enforced.

8. This tax base would require a determination of how to treat loss carry forwards of the CFC from previous years and any losses permitted in a consolidation or group relief regime. If CFC legislation uses the rules of the parent jurisdiction to calculate taxable income, they could also deal with losses in accordance with the rules of the parent jurisdiction (this could mean that a consolidation regime in the CFC jurisdiction would be ignored for purposes of CFC taxation by the parent jurisdiction). If, instead, they use a common standard, then there would need to be a common rule for how losses should be used to calculate taxable income.

   Most countries generally apply their own rules to compute the tax base of the CFC. In principle, however, not all differences in computing the tax base of the CFC under the rules in the CFC and the parent jurisdiction raise the policy concerns that are typically associated with preferential tax provisions or practices that could shrink the tax base for certain income and therefore have the effect of significantly reducing the taxes paid by the CFC. In theory, therefore, CFC rules could take account of only those differences that raise such policy concerns when calculating the tax base of the CFC.

For example, if the tax base in the parent jurisdiction is higher than that in the CFC jurisdiction only because of timing differences in accounting, this may not need to be reflected in the denominator. A participation exemption also may not fall within the scope of tax advantages that are considered in determining the denominator because it is typically granted to eliminate double taxation and not to reduce the actual tax burden. However, the denominator should take into account any differences that are a result of a tax advantage in the CFC jurisdiction insofar as this is merely aimed at attracting offshore capital and therefore increases the risk of profit shifting. A notional interest deduction that has this aim may be an example of such a tax advantage. While it may make sense in theory to differentiate between tax base definitions that implicate the policy concerns underlying CFC rules and those that do not, the only rules that would be likely to make this differentiation are those that start with the tax base calculated under the rules of the CFC jurisdiction and then adjust this upward to reflect the rules of the parent jurisdiction.

Chapter 4

Definition of CFC income

72. This chapter discusses the third CFC building block, which focuses on the definition of CFC income. Once a foreign company has been determined to be a CFC, the next question is whether the income earned by the CFC is of the type that raises concerns and should be attributed to shareholders or controlling parties. CFC rules therefore need to define attributable income, which is also referred to here as "CFC income."

4.1 Recommendation

73. This report recommends that CFC rules should include a definition of income that ensures that income that raises BEPS concerns is attributed to controlling shareholders in the parent jurisdiction. At the same time, it recognises the need for flexibility to ensure that jurisdictions can design CFC rules that are consistent with their domestic policy frameworks. Jurisdictions are free to choose their rules for defining CFC income, including from among the measures set out in the explanation section below. This choice is likely to be dependent on the degree of BEPS risk a jurisdiction faces.

4.2 Explanation

74. This section provides a non-exhaustive list of approaches that CFC rules could use to attribute income that raises BEPS concerns, which may include, among other things, income earned by CFCs that are holding companies, income earned by CFCs that provide financial and banking services, income earned by CFCs that engage in sales invoicing, income from IP assets, income from digital goods and services, and income from captive insurance and re-insurance.[1] These approaches could be applied on their own or combined with each other. CFC rules generally include income that has been separated from the underlying value creation to obtain a reduction in tax. Existing CFC rules use a variety of factors to identify income that raises these concerns. For example, some focus on whether the income is of a type that is more likely to be geographically mobile; some focus on whether the income was earned from or with the assistance of related parties; some focus on the source of the income; and some focus on the level of activity in the CFC. Depending on their policy priorities, different jurisdictions with CFC rules focus on different factors.

75. Regardless of which approach a jurisdiction applies, CFC rules should, at a minimum, capture the funding return allocated under transfer pricing rules to a low-function cash box if that cash box meets the requirements in the previous building blocks (although under CFC regimes that focus on preventing stripping from the parent jurisdiction, the extent of inclusion may depend on how much of the income has been

shifted from the parent jurisdiction).[2] However, as mentioned in Chapter 1, different jurisdictions use CFC rules to achieve different policy outcomes, and an approach that focuses only on funding returns would not be consistent with the policy goals of all jurisdictions. The analyses set out below provide a number of options that could apply more narrowly or that could apply more broadly.[3] Jurisdictions could also apply a full-inclusion system, which would target income raising BEPS concerns by treating all income earned by a CFC as CFC income regardless of its character. Full-inclusion systems also aim to prevent long-term deferral of taxation, which is relevant in the context of worldwide tax systems.

4.2.1 Categorical analysis

76. Existing CFC rules generally apply an analysis that divides income into categories and attributes income differently depending on how it is categorised. Jurisdictions define categories differently depending on which factors or indicia they find most relevant: (i) legal classification, (ii) relatedness of parties, and (iii) source of the income. However, not all income in these categories necessarily raises BEPS concerns.

4.2.1.1 Legal classification

77. Jurisdictions generally first categorise income according to its legal classification, focusing on categories such as the following:[4]

- dividends
- interest
- insurance income
- royalties and IP income
- sales and services income.

78. Jurisdictions that apply a categorical approach based on legal classification separate out these categories of income because they are more likely to be geographically mobile and therefore are likely to raise the concerns that CFC rules are designed to address.

- ***Dividends*** – The general concern underlying the treatment of dividends is that dividends could be used to shift purely “passive” income (i.e. income that does not arise from any underlying activity) into a CFC. However, dividend income typically does not raise such concerns in at least three situations. First, if the dividends were paid out of active income of an affiliate, those dividends may not raise BEPS concerns. Second, many countries now exempt certain dividend income from taxation more generally, and it may not trigger any BEPS concerns to exempt dividends earned by the CFC if those dividends would have been exempted from taxation in the parent jurisdiction had they been earned by the parent company. Third, if the CFC is in the active trade or business of dealing in securities, then dividends paid to that CFC may again not raise concerns if they are linked to the CFC’s trade or business.
- ***Interest*** – The general concern underlying the treatment of interest and financing income is that this income is easy to shift and therefore could have been shifted by the parent into the CFC, possibly leading to overleveraging of the parent and overcapitalisation of the CFC. Interest and financing income is more likely to

raise this concern when it has been earned from related parties, when the CFC is overcapitalised, when the activities contributing to the interest were located outside the CFC jurisdiction, or when the income was not earned from an active financing business. Rules designed to attribute this income should recognise that regulated entities are subject to capitalisation and other requirements, so any rules on overcapitalisation should take account of such requirements and should not attribute income just because an entity is required to maintain a certain level of capital for non-tax purposes.

- ***Insurance income*** – The general concern underlying the treatment of income from the insurance of risks is that profits can be shifted away from jurisdictions in which those risks are located and into a low-tax jurisdiction. Insurance income is more likely to raise these concerns in the following three cases: (i) the CFC was overcapitalised relative to comparable companies in the business of providing insurance; (ii) the policy holder, annuitant, beneficiary, or location of the risks insured were outside the jurisdiction; or (iii) the insurance income was derived from contracts or policies with a related party, particularly if the related party also received a deduction for the payment of the insurance premium. However, income earned by a regulated entity in an insurance group may not raise the same concerns because the regulatory environment sets restrictions in terms of risks and capital.[5]

- ***Royalties and Intellectual Property (IP) income*** – The general concern underlying the treatment of royalties and other income from IP is that, since IP assets are highly mobile, the income from these assets can easily be diverted from the location where the value of the assets was created. IP income (including income from digital goods and services[6]) raises several challenges for CFC rules:

  - IP income is particularly easy to manipulate because it can be exploited and distributed in many different forms, all of which may have different formalistic classifications under the CFC rules of different countries. For instance, income from IP could be embedded in income from sales and therefore treated as active sales income under the CFC rules of some countries.

  - IP assets are often hard to value because there are often no exact comparables, and the cost base of these assets may be an inaccurate measure of the income they can generate.[7]

  - Income that is directly earned from the underlying IP asset is often difficult to separate from the income that is earned from associated services or products.

CFC rules that use a categorical analysis based on legal classification often attempt to address the concerns raised by IP income by separating out royalties and treating them as attributable. Given the challenges above, however, dividing according to legal classification on its own is not enough to attribute all income that does in fact arise out of IP and that raises BEPS concerns.

- ***Sales and services income*** – Income that arises from the sale of goods that were produced in the CFC jurisdiction or from services that were provided in the CFC jurisdiction generally does not raise any concerns about BEPS. Income from sales and services does, however, raise concerns in at least two contexts: (i) invoicing companies; and (ii) IP income. Invoicing companies raise concerns because they earn sales and services income for goods and services that they have purchased from related parties and to which they have added little or no value. As discussed above, income from IP that was shifted into the CFC and to which the CFC has added little to no value is commonly considered as sales and services income and could again escape CFC inclusion. Categorical analyses based on legal classification therefore may not attribute income that raises BEPS concerns if they exclude all sales and services income without taking account of these two situations.

4.2.1.2 Relatedness of parties

79. Some jurisdictions focus on the party from whom income was earned rather than (or along with) the legal classification of the income. Many existing CFC rules include income if it was earned from a related party on the grounds that income is more easily, and more likely to be, shifted in that situation. Some jurisdictions apply a very broad related party test that includes both income from sales to a related party and income from a sale of a good originally purchased from a related party. Another version of a related party rule would apply to income from goods that were developed in conjunction with a related party (e.g., intellectual property that was developed with a related party or as part of a cost-sharing agreement with a related party).[8] All of these use the relatedness of parties as an indicator that income was shifted into the CFC, but they differ based on how much involvement by a related party is enough to ensure that income is attributed.

4.2.1.3 Source of income

80. Some existing CFC rules also categorise income based on where the income was earned. This approach can take the form of either an anti-base-stripping rule or a source-country rule, and the underlying principle is that income that was earned from activities undertaken in the CFC jurisdiction is less likely to raise concerns about profit shifting, while income that was earned from another jurisdiction is more likely to raise such concerns. Anti-base-stripping rules treat income as CFC income if it was earned for sales to a related or unrelated party located in the parent jurisdiction or for services or investments located in the parent jurisdiction. In keeping with the fact that different jurisdictions prioritise different policy objectives, jurisdictions with anti-base-stripping rules may focus on different "types" of base stripping. In jurisdictions that are focused primarily on preventing the stripping of the parent jurisdiction's base, only income generated in the parent jurisdiction will be categorised as CFC income, although this raises the question of how to determine whether income was shifted from the parent jurisdiction. In jurisdictions that are focused on preventing both parent stripping and foreign-to-foreign stripping, however, CFC rules could treat any income generated in a jurisdiction other than the CFC jurisdiction as CFC income. This broader approach would be harder to manipulate than a narrower rule that focuses on just the parent jurisdiction, but it may attribute income that has genuinely been earned from activities carried out by the CFC. Such a situation could arise, for example, where a foreign company that previously had customers in the parent jurisdiction became a CFC when it was purchased as part of a merger or acquisition. A broad anti-base-stripping rule could also take the form of a source-country rule, which excludes highly mobile income from CFC income if it was earned in the CFC jurisdiction.

4.2.2 Substance analysis

81. A substance analysis looks to whether the CFC engaged in substantial activities in determining what income is CFC income. Many existing CFC rules apply a substance analysis of some sort, and many Member States of the European Union combine a categorical approach with a carve-out for genuine economic activities. Substance analyses can use a variety of proxies to determine whether the CFC's income was separated from the underlying substance, including people, premises, assets, and risks. Regardless of which proxies they consider, substance analyses are generally asking the same fundamental question, which is whether the CFC had the ability to earn the income itself. Substance analyses could be combined with the categorical or excess profits analysis, and most existing substance analyses apply alongside more mechanical rules and are not stand-alone rules. Although such rules add to the complexity of CFC rules, they may be more able to accurately identify and quantify shifted income.

82. A substance analysis can apply as either a threshold test or a proportionate analysis. Under a threshold (or "all-or-nothing") test, a set amount of activity (as identified through one or more proxies) would allow all income of the CFC to be excluded. A CFC that had not engaged in this amount of activity would have all of its income included in CFC income. Under a proportionate analysis, CFC income would only exclude the amount of income that was proportionate to the amount of activity that the CFC had undertaken. For example, if the CFC had undertaken 75% of the activity that would have to in fact be performed to earn the CFC's income, then 25% of its income would be treated as CFC income. This could increase the administrative complexity and compliance costs of the rules,[9] but it should prevent businesses from locating just the right type and amount of activity in a CFC to ensure that its profits are excluded by the CFC rules of its parent jurisdiction. One further advantage of applying a substance test on a proportionate basis is that it is more likely to comply with EU law because it would allow CFC rules to attribute only the income that does not arise from genuine economic activities

83. As discussed in Chapter 1, one of the policy considerations underlying the design of CFC rules is how to limit administrative and compliance burdens while not creating opportunities for avoidance. Substance analyses highlight this consideration since they typically rely on more qualitative measures than categorical analyses, and they are often included in CFC rules because they may be more accurate than a purely mechanical approach. Their inclusion, however, could lead to increased administrative and compliance burdens. This is because they require an analysis of the CFC's facts and circumstances. However, the incremental burden may be small because this analysis may be similar to that required for transfer pricing purposes. Where this analysis reveals that the CFC has insufficient substance, some or all of its profits, even after any transfer pricing adjustments, may be included in CFC income.

84. However, substance analyses can be designed to address these concerns and to apply more mechanically while still increasing the accuracy of purely objective analyses. One possible response would be to use a substance analysis only for certain narrow categories of income, so that income in other categories was either automatically included or automatically excluded depending on its categorisation. This approach could, at minimum, not apply a substance test to categories of income that jurisdictions considered to be automatically attributable because of their mobility, the relatedness of parties, or their source. A second response would be to apply a substance analysis as a threshold test

instead of as a proportionate test. A third response would be to consider objective factors such as expenditures rather than factors that are harder to measure.[10]

85. Recognising the concerns about complexity and interactions with transfer pricing rules, there are many different ways that a jurisdiction could design a substance analysis that is consistent with the jurisdiction's policy objectives, including the options listed below:

- One option would be a threshold test that applies a facts and circumstances analysis to determine whether the employees of the CFC have made a substantial contribution to the income earned by the CFC.[11] This option could be designed to include certain safe harbours, ratios, or other more mechanical tests that determine whether there has been a substantial contribution.
- A second option would look at all the significant functions performed by entities within the group to determine whether the CFC is the entity which would be most likely to own particular assets, or undertake particular risks, if the entities were unrelated.[12] If this were a threshold test, it would treat as CFC income all income of a CFC that fell below the threshold of significant functions (or exclude all income of a CFC that had the required functions). If it were a proportionate test, it would treat as CFC income only that income that the CFC did not have the significant functions necessary to earn.
- A third option would consider whether the CFC had the necessary business premises and establishment in the CFC jurisdiction to actually earn the income and whether the CFC had the necessary number of employees with the requisite skills in the CFC jurisdiction to undertake the majority of the CFC's core functions.[13] If applied as a threshold test, this would attribute all the income of a CFC that did not have the necessary people and premises (or exclude all the income of a CFC that did have the necessary people and premises). If applied as a proportionate test, this would treat as CFC income all the income that the CFC did not have the people and premises to earn.
- A fourth option that would be a variation on the third option and that would maintain consistency with work done in other areas of the BEPS Project would use the nexus approach that was developed in the context of Action Item 5 to ensure that preferential IP regimes require substantial activity.[14] CFC rules could include a version of the nexus approach as a substance analysis, under which income earned by the CFC that met the requirements of the nexus approach would not be included in CFC income, while all other income from qualifying IP assets as defined by the nexus approach would be treated as CFC income. Under this version of the nexus approach, all IP income from qualifying IP assets would be attributed unless the taxpayer could show that the income would qualify for benefits under a nexus-compliant IP regime in the CFC jurisdiction. If the CFC jurisdiction did not operate a nexus-compliant IP regime, then this could apply to all income arising from a qualifying IP asset that was either acquired from or developed with a related party, and all such income would be attributed unless the taxpayer could show that it would qualify for benefits under the terms of the nexus approach itself. As this option would only apply to income arising from qualifying IP assets, it may need to be combined with another substance analysis for other types of income (including other IP income).

86. Substance analyses generally increase the accuracy of CFC rules, but this increased accuracy must be weighed against the increased complexity and expense of more fact-intensive substance analyses. Depending on their policy objectives, some jurisdictions may prioritise accuracy over simplicity, but others may design their rules to make their substance analyses more mechanical and less complex.

4.2.3 Excess profits analysis

87. Another approach to defining income is an "excess profits" analysis, which is not a feature of any existing CFC rules. This would characterise income in excess of a "normal return" earned in low tax jurisdictions as CFC income. Such an approach could, for instance, be relevant in the context of IP income as generally taxpayers cannot expect to earn a profit in excess of the normal returns from simply purchasing and selling and providing services or manufacturing, unless those activities involve the use of IP. In certain situations, intangibles and risk-shifting transactions among related parties could be susceptible to systematic mispricing, leading to a profit in excess of the normal returns that would not occur if the same transactions were undertaken with unrelated parties. This should mean that an excess profits approach will tend to apply to income from intangibles and risk shifting.

88. Depending on their policy objectives, jurisdictions could include a specific entry criterion so that the excess profits approach would only apply in situations in which the CFC made use of intangible property acquired from or developed by or with the assistance of a related party, which means this approach could be combined with categorical analyses. Alternatively, this approach could be combined with a prove-out under which the excess profits approach would apply to all CFCs *unless* they could show that they did not make use of any intangible property acquired from or developed by or with the assistance of a related party.[15] Jurisdictions with different policy objectives could, however, not apply an entry criterion or a kick-out and could instead apply the excess profits analysis to all income earned by the CFC.

89. The proposed excess profits analysis calculates the normal return and then subtracts this normal return from the income earned by the CFC. The difference is the excess return, all of which is treated as CFC income. The normal return means the return that a normal investor would expect to make with respect to an equity investment. This normal return could be calculated using the following formula:

normal return = (rate of return) x (eligible equity)

90. This formula requires a determination, first, of what rate of return to use and, second, of how to calculate eligible equity.

- ***Rate of return*** – In terms of *rate of return*, normal investors are unlikely to accept a risk-free rate of return with respect to an investment with an uncertain income stream. The normal rate of return with respect to an equity investment therefore should be a *risk-inclusive rate of return* that equals *the risk-free rate of return plus a premium reflecting the risk associated with an equity investment*, although some jurisdictions may use the risk-free rate of return depending on their policy objectives. Economic studies often estimate the risk-inclusive rate as being approximately 8% to 10%, although this varies by industry, leverage, and jurisdiction.[16]

- ***Eligible equity*** – As the excess profits approach is intended to provide an exemption for normal returns from assets used in connection with the actual functions carried out in a low-tax jurisdiction, then only equity invested in assets used in the active conduct of a trade or business, including IP assets, should be treated as eligible equity. As income subject to taxation under other CFC rules in the parent jurisdiction would not be included in total returns, jurisdictions could exclude from eligible equity any equity invested in assets that produced income that had been subject to taxation under other CFC rules in the parent jurisdiction.[17]

91. The normal return would then be subtracted from all income earned by the CFC that was not subject to taxation under other CFC rules in the parent jurisdiction. The excess would be included in CFC income.

92. For an example of how the excess profits analysis would work, imagine that Sub B, located in Country B, is a wholly owned subsidiary of Parent, which is located in Country A. Sub B uses its manufacturing facilities in Country B to manufacture and distribute Product B, which uses IP purchased from Parent. In Year 1, Sub B spent 600 000 to purchase the rights to IP developed by Parent, and Sub B also invested a total of 500 000 in its manufacturing facilities. For book purposes, the acquisition of the IP and the investment in manufacturing facilities result in assets on the balance sheet with a value equal to the acquisition costs. Both the IP and the manufacturing facilities are used in Sub B's active trade or business of manufacturing and distributing Product B. In Year 2, Sub B earned 700 000 in profits from sales of Product B.[18] To determine whether Sub B has attributable income, the excess profits analysis would calculate normal returns using the following formula:

normal return = (rate of return) x (eligible equity)

93. If the rate of return for the excess profits approach had been set at 10%, then that formula would show that the normal return was 110 000 per year. (This is because 110 000 = 10% x (600 000 + 500 000.) The excess returns would then be calculated by subtracting 110,000 from Sub B's profits. Sub B's excess returns for Year 2 would therefore be 590 000, and all of this income would be treated as attributable income.

94. An excess profits approach would not rely on formal classification to determine whether income was included; it would not be necessary to consider where or from whom, or from which activities income was earned; and it should not lead to income that does not raise BEPS concerns sheltering income that does. However, the mechanical nature of this approach must be weighed against whether it could target shifted income with sufficient accuracy and challenges with quantifying the normal return. Depending on policy objectives, some countries that prioritise accuracy over a mechanical rule consider that the excess profits approach must be combined with a mandatory substance-based exclusion. Other countries may consider that excluding a normal return on eligible equity is an effective method for identifying CFC income. Because of these concerns, there is no consensus on whether the excess profits approach should be combined with a mandatory substance-based exclusion.

4.2.4 Transactional and entity approaches

95. Regardless of which type of analysis they use to define CFC income, jurisdictions need to determine whether to apply this analysis on an entity-by-entity basis

or on a transactional basis, which would attribute individual streams of income. Under the entity approach, an entity that does not earn a certain amount or percentage of attributable income or an entity that engages in certain activities will be found not to have any attributable income, even if some of its income would be of an attributable character. Under the transactional approach, in contrast, the character of each stream of income is assessed to determine whether that stream of income is attributable. The difference between the two approaches is that, under the entity approach, either all or none of the income will be included depending on whether the majority falls within the definition of CFC income. Under the transactional approach, some income can still be included even if the majority does not fall within the definition of CFC income, and some income can be excluded even if the majority does fall within this definition.

96. The entity approach may reduce administrative burdens in certain situations because, once tax administrations have determined either that a certain amount of income earned by an entity is attributable or that the entity engaged in a certain level of activity, CFC rules are either applicable or not and no further analysis needs to be undertaken. The entity approach could also reduce taxpayer compliance costs and increase certainty because taxpayers know that they will only be subject to CFC tax if a significant portion of their income falls within the definition of attributable income. The entity approach thus reduces the chances that a taxpayer will be subject to CFC rules if CFC income makes up only a small portion of its overall income. However, the main disadvantage of the entity approach is that, by subjecting either all or none of an entity's income to CFC rules, it is both over-inclusive and under-inclusive. An entity that earns enough CFC income will have all its income attributed (including income that would not otherwise be attributable), while an entity with some income that would otherwise be included may be able to escape CFC rules by swamping that income with income that is not subject to the CFC rules. For example, an entity that engages primarily in activities that generate active income may be able to shield a large amount of passive income from CFC rules.[19] Also, the entity approach may not reduce administrative burdens significantly, since this approach still requires taxpayers to determine whether individual streams of income are attributable or not, but they may not have to make this determination for all income streams once they have determined whether they fall above or below the entity threshold.

97. The transactional approach may increase administrative burdens and compliance costs relative to the entity approach, and it may require tax administrations to consider a larger number of companies under their CFC rules, depending on how other elements of those rules are designed. For instance, if CFC rules set too high a threshold when considering if a CFC is lowly taxed and apply a proportionate substance analysis, they may bring a large number of companies within the scope of CFC rules and this may be compounded if they also apply CFC rules on a transactional basis. Despite these disadvantages, the transactional approach is generally more accurate at attributing income. As a transactional approach requires consideration of each stream of income to determine whether it falls within the definition of CFC income it is better able to target specific types of income more effectively than the entity approach. It is also possible to attribute only that income that raises BEPS concerns, and this greater proportionality suggests that the transactional approach may be more consistent with both the goals of Action Item 3 and EU law.[20] Transactional approaches may, however, require a threshold to ensure that active businesses that hold a cash surplus do not have to treat the income from that cash surplus as CFC income. This threshold could be a bright-line de minimis threshold. In Australia, for example, none of the income of a CFC is attributed if 5% or less of that CFC's income is passive income. Alternatively, CFC rules could require a

functional analysis to determine how much otherwise attributable income is in fact being held as a cash surplus. The first type of threshold would reduce administrative burdens and compliance costs but may not be accurate in all situations, while the second type of threshold would be more accurate but would increase administrative burdens and compliance costs.[21]

Notes

1. Some of these categories of income are discussed in greater detail in paragraph 78.

2. See the 2015 Report on Action 8-10: *Aligning Transfer Pricing Outcomes With Value Creation* (OECD, 2015) which allocates a risk-free financial return to an entity that lacks the ability to control risks.

3. Note that not all of these analyses automatically capture the funding return allocated to a low-function cash box, but they could all be designed to do so. The categorical analysis, for example, could be designed to include such a funding return in a category that was automatically attributed, regardless of the legal classification of the funding return.

4. Jurisdictions could also include other categories of income, such as rents and leasing fees.

5. For example, CFC rules that attribute insurance income could exclude income from reinsurance activities that meet all or most of the following features:

    - The reinsurance contract is priced on arms-length terms.
    - There is diversification and pooling of risk in the reinsurer.
    - The economic capital position of the group has improved as a result of diversification and there is therefore a real economic impact for the group as a whole.
    - Both the insurer and reinsurer are regulated entities with broadly similar regulatory regimes and regulators that require evidence of risk transfer and appropriate capital levels.
    - The original insurance involves third party risks outside the group.
    - The CFC has the requisite skills and experience at its disposal, including employees in the CFC or a related service company with senior underwriting expertise.
    - The CFC has a real possibility of suffering losses.

6. The digital economy cannot generally be defined separately from other parts of the economy, but the value of digital goods and services is typically due to intellectual property. In the context of both general IP income and digital goods and services, there is not always an identifiable IP asset, but income earned in both contexts is typically due to IP of some sort. Income from digital goods and services is therefore not considered a separate category of income but rather a subset of IP income in this report.

7. See Public Discussion Draft on BEPS Action Item 8: Hard-to-Value Intangibles (OECD, 4 June 2015), available at www.oecd.org/ctp/transfer-pricing/discussion-draft-beps-action-8-hard-to-value-intangibles.pdf. At paragraph 9, the Discussion Draft defines hard-to-value intangibles to include "intangibles or rights in intangibles for which, at the time of their transfer in a transaction between associated enterprises, (i) no sufficiently reliable comparables exist; and (ii) there is a lack of reliable projections of future cashflows or income expected to be derived from the five transferred intangible, or the assumptions used in valuing the intangible are highly uncertain."

8. Such a rule was proposed by the US administration as part of its definition of foreign base company digital income in 2015.

9. As discussed below, a proportionate substance analysis that considers more mechanical factors, such as expenditures, may not raise these same administrative and compliance issues. More mechanical proportionate approaches, however, are looking at proxies for substantial activities, so they may not always be accurate in their attribution.

10. These possible responses, particularly the first and second, may be less appropriate for Member States of the European Union.

11. One example of this first option is the U.S. CFC rules. Under the substantial contribution test that applies to sales income earned by a CFC, income from the sale of personal property that would normally be treated as attributable will not be attributable if "the facts and circumstances evince that the controlled foreign corporation makes a substantial contribution through the activities of its employees to the manufacture, production, or construction of the personal property sold". 26 CFR 1.954-3(a)(4)(iv)(a). The test then provides a list of seven activities that could indicate that the CFC did make a substantial contribution, all of which essentially consider whether the CFC was engaged in actual value creation. These activities include (1) oversight and direction of the activities or process pursuant to which the property is manufactured, produced, or constructed; (2) activities that are considered in determining whether the products were substantially transformed or if the assembly or conversion of component parts into a final product are substantial in nature and generally considered to constitute the manufacture, production, or construction of property; (3) material selection, vendor selection, or control of the raw materials, work-in-process or finished goods; (4) management of manufacturing costs or capacities (for example, managing the risk of loss, cost reduction or efficiency initiatives associated with the manufacturing process, demand planning, production scheduling, or hedging raw material costs); (5) control of manufacturing related logistics; (6) quality control (for example, sample testing or establishment of quality control standards); and (7) developing, or directing the use or development of, product design and design specifications, as well as trade secrets, technology, or other intellectual property for the purpose of manufacturing, producing, or constructing the personal property. 26 CFR 1.954-3(a)(4)(iv)(b). The Regulations then provide examples to illustrate how this facts and circumstances test would apply.

12. An example of the second option can be found in the UK's CFC rules, which has used the concepts and guidance developed by the OECD for Article 7 to identify the group's significant people functions associated with each asset, so that it can be determined whether the CFC undertakes those functions.

13. An example of the third option is the South African foreign business establishment test. Under this test, income of a CFC is not attributable if it is produced by a foreign

business establishment (FBE) that operates at arm's length. FBEs are places of business with a physical structure that are used (or will continue to be used) for at least one year. These places of business must be where the business of the CFC is undertaken and they must be suitably equipped and staffed with managerial and operational employees who render services for the purpose of conducting the CFC's primary operations.

14. The nexus approach applies a proportionate analysis to income, under which the proportion of income that may benefit from an IP regime is the same proportion as that between qualifying expenditures (i.e. expenditures incurred for Research and Development (R&D) undertaken by the CFC or unrelated parties) and overall expenditures (i.e. qualifying expenditures plus acquisition costs and expenditures incurred for R&D undertaken by related parties). Under the nexus approach, R&D expenditures are used as a proxy for substantial activities, and they provide a more mechanical way of determining whether the CFC had the necessary people to earn the IP income itself.

15. If either of these provisions were included, intangible property would be defined broadly to mean something which is not a physical asset or a financial asset, which is capable of being owned or controlled for use in commercial activities, and which increases the value received by the company, over and above normal returns. Under this definition, intangible property should include intangibles that are not legally protected, such as trade secrets, know-how, customer lists, management systems, networks, data, goodwill, and other similar items. This approach could be combined with a source country rule, which would allow income that was earned from the market of the CFC jurisdiction (e.g., from customers in the CFC jurisdiction or for services provided in the CFC jurisdiction) to be excluded from the excess profits calculation.

16. The risk-free rate of return varies by country, and it can generally be calculated by reference to an average of the government bond rate over several years. Although it may at first appear sensible to use the risk-free rate of return in the CFC jurisdiction, the principle underlying CFC rules is that the parent company has the influence to determine where the CFC is located (and whether income is shifted to it). The parent company is therefore likely to make its investment decisions based on the rate of return in the parent jurisdiction. The risk-free rate of return used to calculate the risk-inclusive rate of return could therefore be based on that in the parent jurisdiction. The equity premium represents the additional expected return an investor requires in order to be compensated for the uncertainty of the return from a particular investment. Economic analysis has not conclusively determined what an appropriate equity premium would be, but it varies across industries and depends on the leverage of the company, and it is often calculated as being between 3% and 7%.

17. In terms of how to calculate the equity invested in these assets, one option would be to use the book value of eligible assets less the liabilities apportioned to the eligible equity. Book value may sometimes be a more accurate measure than historic costs, but in other cases, assets are expensed as they are created and therefore not recognised on the balance sheet at all. Another option would be to use tax basis or tax acquisition cost for the valuation, as determined under the law of the parent jurisdiction. Liabilities would need to be apportioned, most likely based on relative asset values or earnings, potentially with the ability to trace liabilities associated with non-recourse debt.

18. For ease of calculation, this example assumes that there are no liabilities apportioned to the manufacturing facilities.

19. EU Member States may need to consider whether an entity approach is consistent with EU law.

20. Although the European Court of Justice (ECJ) has not yet considered genuine economic activities on a transaction-by-transaction basis, it appears that CFC rules that attribute income on a transactional basis would be more narrowly focused on income that raises concerns and therefore may be more consistent with EU law.

21. Some jurisdictions combine these two approaches into a hybrid approach and first determine whether an entity has a sufficient amount of attributable income to be treated as a CFC before assessing whether specific items of income are to be attributed. Japan's CFC rules provide an example of such a hybrid approach, under which certain entities are excluded from CFC taxation due to the type of income and activities, but certain streams of income earned by those entities may still be subject to CFC taxation. Because this approach ultimately considers different streams of income rather than just attributing all the income of an entity, it is essentially a version of a transactional approach.

Bibliography

OECD (2015), *Aligning Transfer Pricing Outcomes with Value Creation, Actions 8-10 - 2015 Final Reports*, OECD/G20 Base Erosion and Profit Shifting Project, OECD Publishing, Paris, http://dx.doi.org/10.1787/9789264241244-en.

Chapter 5

Rules for computing income

98. This chapter sets out recommendations for the fourth CFC building block on computing income. Once CFC rules have determined that income is attributable, they must then consider how much income to attribute.

5.1 Recommendations

99. Computing the income of a CFC requires two different determinations: (i) which jurisdiction's rules should apply; and (ii) whether any specific rules for computing CFC income are necessary. The recommendation for the first determination is to use the rules of the parent jurisdiction to calculate a CFC's income. The recommendation for the second determination is that, to the extent legally permitted, jurisdictions should have a specific rule limiting the offset of CFC losses so that they can only be used against the profits of the same CFC or against the profits of other CFCs in the same jurisdiction.

5.2 Explanation

100. The first recommendation focuses on rules that are used to calculate taxable income. Four options were considered to arrive at the first recommendation.

1. One option would be to apply the law of the parent jurisdiction (i.e., the jurisdiction that is applying the CFC rules), which would be logically consistent with BEPS concerns particularly if CFC rules focus on the erosion of the parent jurisdiction's tax base. This option would also reduce costs for the tax administration. Jurisdictions could achieve a broadly similar outcome by starting with the income calculated according to the rules of the CFC jurisdiction and then adjusting the income in line with the rules of the parent jurisdiction.
2. A second option would be to use the CFC jurisdiction's rules for computing income, but this would be inconsistent with the goals of Action Item 3 as using the CFC jurisdiction's rules may allow for less income to be attributed. This could also create complexity and increase the administration costs for the tax administration that would have to apply unfamiliar rules.
3. A third option would be to allow taxpayers to choose either jurisdiction's computational rules, but this is likely to create opportunities for tax planning.
4. A final option would be to compute income using a common standard. For example, some jurisdictions instruct taxpayers to use the International Financial Reporting Standards (IFRS). The advantage of this option is that it could in theory lead to international consistency as all CFCs and parent jurisdictions would be

using the same rules for calculating CFC income, regardless of the residence of either the CFC or the parent. Since most countries do not currently use such standards when calculating taxable income, however, this option may increase both administrative and compliance costs if taxpayers have to recalculate the income of the CFC according to standards that are applied by neither the parent jurisdiction nor the CFC jurisdiction.

101. Based on this analysis, the first option is recommended because it is consistent with the goals of the *BEPS Action Plan* (OECD, 2013) and it reduces administrative costs.

102. In arriving at the second recommendation, the question of how to treat losses was considered. Most issues involving losses can be addressed by reference to pre-existing domestic laws in the parent jurisdiction.[1] These include questions about whether the use of losses should be limited to offset against profits of a similar character, which would mean that, for example, passive losses of a CFC could only be used against passive profits if that limit applied in domestic laws on losses.

103. Another issue is whether CFC losses should only be offset against CFC profits or whether they can also be used against profits in the parent company. Most existing CFC rules only allow the losses of the CFC to be offset against the profits of that CFC or CFCs in the same jurisdiction, and this is the recommended approach since allowing CFC losses to be offset against the profits of parent companies or CFCs in other jurisdictions could encourage manipulation of losses in the CFC jurisdiction.[2] However this may not be an issue that is already dealt with in rules that apply in the domestic context, so a separate CFC-specific rule may be required. A rule that prevents CFC losses being set off against non-CFC profits could apply alongside a rule that limits the offset of losses to similar types of profits so that passive losses of a CFC could only be offset against passive profits of that same CFC. Any concerns about over-taxation resulting from this approach could be mitigated by allowing CFC losses to be carried forwards or backwards for use against profits arising in other years if such treatment is otherwise permitted under the laws of the parent jurisdiction[3].

104. The recommendation on loss limitation can be illustrated with the following example. Parent is a resident in Country A and Sub B is a wholly owned subsidiary in Country B that is a CFC. Country A has CFC rules. In year 1, Parent earns 1000 and Sub B earns 500 of CFC income. Parent has 200 in losses and Sub B has 1000 in losses. This is illustrated in Figure 5.1.

Figure 5.1 Loss limitation

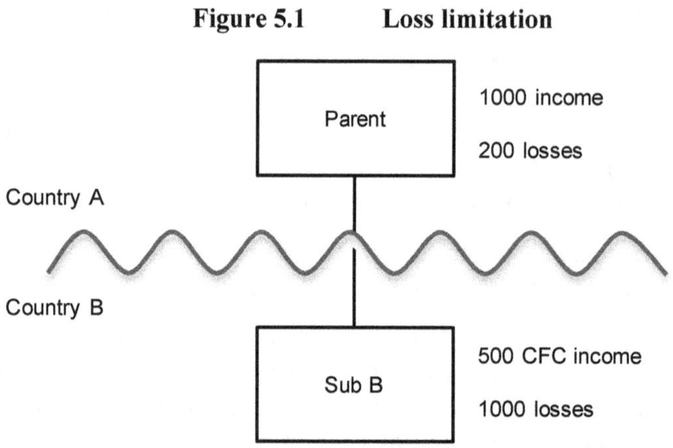

105. If Country A's CFC rules do not limit the losses of Sub B to the income of Sub B, then Parent will only be taxed on 300 because the full 1200 of losses will be offset against the full 1500 of income. If, however, Country A's CFC rules do limit the losses of Sub B to the income of Sub B, then Parent will be taxed on 800 (1000 - 200), and no income will be attributed to Parent from Sub B because all of Sub B's attributable income will be offset by the losses, and the remaining 500 could potentially, depending on Country A's CFC rules, be carried forward to be used against Sub B's future income. This limit will prevent use of CFCs to reduce the taxable income in the parent jurisdiction.

106. If Country A already has a rule that does not permit passive losses to offset active income, this rule can be combined with the recommended loss limitation as shown in Figure 5.2.

Figure 5.2 Loss limitation with pre-existing passive limitation

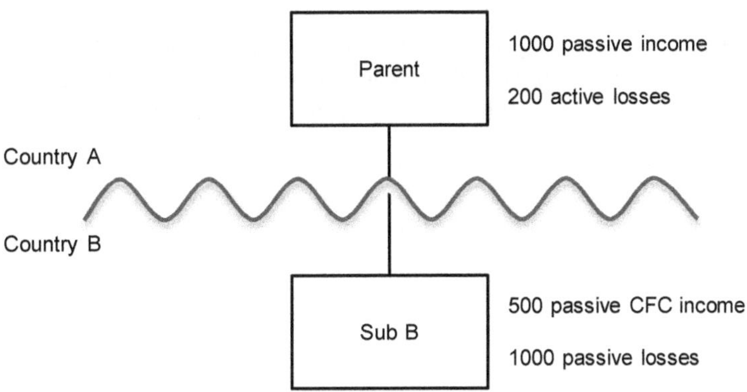

107. If all of Parent's income is passive and all of Parent's losses are active, while all of Sub B's income and losses are passive, Parent would be taxed on 1000 of its income. This is because Parent's active losses could not be used against its passive income and because Sub B's passive losses would offset all of its passive income, and the excess passive losses could not be used to offset Parent's income under the CFC loss limitation rule.

108. Another concern is potential loss importation. This concern could arise if a CFC has losses that date from before its characterisation as a CFC or if another activity bearing losses is transferred to the CFC to soak up profits. If losses are only available to be offset against CFC profits then the fact that the CFC incurred losses in prior years may not be a problem. However, there may be concerns if the activity of the CFC has changed and there is evidence that either profits or losses have been shifted to the CFC to reduce the amount of income that is ultimately taxed. Many countries have domestic law provisions designed to prevent tax avoidance that deal with these situations and these could equally be applied to the CFC's computation of income.

Notes

1. Using domestic law provisions to answer questions about the treatment of specific items such as losses would create complications if CFC income is generally calculated using the laws of a different jurisdiction but this is another reason supporting the use of the parent jurisdiction's rules and the first recommendation above.

2. Jurisdictions could also implement rules permitting parent company losses to be used against CFC profits. This situation is less likely to raise BEPS concerns since this would lead to fewer losses in the parent company and fewer profits in the CFC.

3. Member States of the European Union should determine whether a restriction of CFC losses would be consistent with the fundamental freedoms of the European Union as considered in Chapter 1.

Bibliography

OECD (2013), *Action Plan on Base Erosion and Profit Shifting*, OECD Publishing, Paris, http://dx.doi.org/10.1787/9789264202719-en.

Chapter 6

Rules for attributing income

109. This chapter sets out recommendations for the fifth CFC building block on attributing income. Once the amount of CFC income has been calculated, the next step is determining how to attribute that income to the appropriate shareholders in the CFC.

6.1 Recommendations

110. Income attribution can be broken into five steps: (i) determining which taxpayers should have income attributed to them; (ii) determining how much income should be attributed; (iii) determining when the income should be included in the returns of the taxpayers; (iv) determining how the income should be treated; and (v) determining what tax rate should apply to the income.

111. The recommendations for these steps are as follows:

1. The attribution threshold should be tied to the minimum control threshold when possible, although countries can choose to use different attribution and control thresholds depending on the policy considerations underlying CFC rules.
2. The amount of income to be attributed to each shareholder or controlling person should be calculated by reference to both their proportion of ownership and their actual period of ownership or influence (influence could for instance be based on ownership on the last day of the year if that accurately captures the level of influence).

3. and 4. Jurisdictions can determine when income should be included in taxpayers' returns and how it should be treated so that CFC rules operate in a way that is coherent with existing domestic law.

5. CFC rules should apply the tax rate of the parent jurisdiction to the income.[1]

6.2 Explanation

112. In arriving at the above recommendations, each of the five steps was considered in greater detail.

6.2.1 Which taxpayers should income be attributed to?

113. In order to attribute income correctly, jurisdictions must first determine to whom the income is to be attributed. Many existing CFC rules tie this determination to the earlier determination of control, so that, if a taxpayer met the minimum control threshold, then that taxpayer would also have income attributed to it. In jurisdictions that apply a concentrated

ownership rule, CFC income is generally attributed not just to taxpayers who meet the overall control threshold but also to all resident taxpayers who have the minimum level of control (e.g., 10%) to be considered when calculating whether the control threshold has been met. The benefits of tying the attribution threshold to the minimum control threshold include administrative simplicity and reduced compliance burdens. This also ensures that taxpayers have enough influence to gather information on the activities and income of the CFC. However, using control rules to determine attribution could potentially lead to under-inclusion if it is believed that a minority ownership could in fact have sufficient influence over the business decisions of a CFC to raise Base Erosion and Profit Shifting (BEPS) concerns, but this disadvantage can be reduced if the control rules aggregate the interests of minority shareholders or otherwise do not limit control to majority owners.

114. Some CFC rules may, however, use a different rule to determine which taxpayers have CFC income attributed to them, based on the theory that the amount of ownership that is sufficient for control may not be the same as the level that is sufficient for attribution. Jurisdictions that want to deter even minority investments in CFCs may use a lower attribution threshold, while those that are instead focused on deterring investments by residents that can influence the CFC may set their attribution threshold higher than their control threshold, particularly if their control threshold considers concentrated ownership. Further, CFC rules that look at de facto control or otherwise establish control in a less mechanical way may need to have different control and attribution tests to ensure that the correct taxpayers have income attributed to them. Although having separate rules for attribution and control may in theory create additional compliance costs or administrative burdens, actual attribution of profits may only occur relatively infrequently due to the deterrent nature of CFC rules. Best practice would therefore be either to tie the attribution threshold to the control threshold or to use another attribution threshold that attributed income to, at minimum, taxpayers who could influence the CFC.

6.2.2 How much income should be attributed?

115. Once CFC rules have determined which taxpayers will have income attributed to them, they must then determine how much of that income to attribute. All existing CFC rules attribute income in proportion to each taxpayer's ownership, but they differ in how they treat taxpayers whose ownership lasted for only a portion of the year. Some jurisdictions attribute the entire portion of income based on ownership on the last day of the year. Whilst this could lead to inaccurate attribution and could create opportunities for tax planning, this may accurately capture whether or not the taxpayer was able to influence the CFC if voting or other power is determined based on ownership on the last day of the year or if there are other anti-abuse rules to prevent inappropriate under-attribution of profits. Other jurisdictions attribute income based on the period of ownership, which results in taxpayers being taxed on an amount that is similar to their actual share of the CFC profits. In addition, applying such a rule appears unlikely to add significant compliance costs in practice.[2] Either of these approaches to determining how much income should be attributed can qualify as best practice so long as the determination based on the last day of the year accurately captures the taxpayer's influence.[3]

116. Attribution rules should also ensure that it is not possible to attribute more than 100% of the income of the CFC. This situation could arise, for example, where legal control and economic control together led to more than 100% control. Any rule designed to prevent over-attribution, however, should include anti-avoidance provisions to ensure that it is not used to prevent taxpayers from having an amount attributed to them that accurately captures their influence.

6.2.3 When should the income be included in tax returns?

117. Many existing CFC rules specify that the attributed income must be included in the taxpayer's taxable income for the taxable year in which the end of the CFC's accounting period ends, although some countries have slightly different rules for determining the year in which the attributed income should be included. Korea's CFC rules, for example, state that the attributed income will be included on the return for the taxable year to which the 60th day from the end of the CFC's fiscal year belongs. Both approaches seem equally effective at combatting BEPS, so there is no recommendation for this step and countries are free to adopt provisions that ensure that CFC rules are coherent with general domestic law provisions.

6.2.4 How should the income be treated?

118. A further question to be answered when attributing income to taxpayers is how that income will be treated in the parent jurisdiction. Existing CFC rules take several different approaches, including treating attributed income as a deemed dividend or treating it as having been earned by the taxpayer directly (i.e., the CFC is essentially treated as a partnership or flow-through entity but only for the purposes of attributing CFC income). If attributed income is treated as a deemed dividend, then the tax treatment can build on existing dividend rules with which taxpayers and tax administrations are already familiar. However jurisdictions may not want to treat attributed income as a deemed dividend for all tax purposes and therefore the limit of any "deeming" will need to be made clear. In contrast, treating attributed income as if it were earned directly by shareholders of the CFC is likely to reduce the need for any separate characterisation rules since the income will be characterised according to existing domestic rules. Both approaches seem equally appropriate in terms of dealing with BEPS and therefore the question of how to treat attributed income could be left for jurisdictions to decide in a manner that is coherent with domestic law.

6.2.5 What tax rate should apply to CFC income?

119. Finally, attribution of income raises the question of how that income is taxed once it is attributed. Whilst existing CFC rules subject CFC income to taxation at the rate that would apply to the parent company in the parent jurisdiction, a second option would be to apply a "top-up tax". A top-up tax, which builds closely on the concept of a minimum tax, would only subject CFC income to the difference between the tax paid and a set threshold. This threshold could be tied to the tax rate exemption used to determine whether CFC rules apply to a given CFC, or it could be an entirely separate threshold. A top-up tax would set a floor for the rate at which CFC income is taxed.

120. To illustrate how a top-up tax could work, imagine a parent jurisdiction with a flat 30% statutory tax rate and a CFC rule that applied only to CFCs that were subject to an effective tax rate of less than 12%. If the parent jurisdiction applied a top-up tax to a CFC that was subject to a 0% effective tax rate, it would only tax the CFC income at 12%, instead of its normal rate of 30%. This approach could mean that Multinational Corporations (MNCs) located in higher-tax jurisdictions with CFC rules would not be at a competitive disadvantage relative to MNCs located in some lower-tax jurisdictions. However, they would remain at a competitive disadvantage compared to both MNCs located in jurisdictions with CFC rules but with a tax rate below the top-up tax rate and MNCs located in jurisdictions without CFC rules. The top-up tax would also not necessarily eliminate incentives to shift profits away from higher tax jurisdictions. For instance, in the example above, MNCs located in the parent jurisdiction would have a considerable incentive to shift their income into the CFC

jurisdiction because the maximum rate at which they would be taxed on their CFC income would be 12%, so 18 percentage points lower than the rate that would apply if their income were earned in the parent jurisdiction. The top-up tax may therefore not be consistent with all policy objectives that jurisdictions use their CFC rules to achieve. For some jurisdictions, however, it could be seen as a middle way that would enable jurisdictions to address some degree of competitiveness concerns. If the level set for the top-up tax rate was the same as that as the tax rate exemption, it may also make CFC rules more internally consistent.

Notes

1. To limit competitiveness concerns, countries could also consider a top-up tax. This may be more appropriate where a more approximate or mechanical rule could potentially capture active income. See paragraphs 119-120 for a more detailed explanation of a top-up tax.
2. It is assumed that such a rule would attribute income if the taxpayer held an interest in the CFC for a portion of the year but did not hold that interest on the last day of the year. If not, the recommended rule could be combined with a rule for imputing CFC income when CFC shares are disposed of in the middle of the year.
3. One possible way of capturing influence would be to combine a rule that considers ownership on the last day of the year with reporting requirements on ownership throughout the year.

Chapter 7

Rules to prevent or eliminate double taxation

121. This chapter sets out recommendations for the sixth and final CFC building block on rules to prevent or eliminate double taxation. As discussed in Chapter 1, one of the fundamental policy considerations raised by CFC rules is how to ensure that these rules do not lead to double taxation, which could pose an obstacle to international competitiveness, growth and economic development.

7.1 Recommendations

122. CFC rules should include provisions to ensure that the application of these rules does not lead to double taxation. There are at least three situations where double taxation may arise: (i) situations where the attributed CFC income is also subject to foreign corporate taxes; (ii) situations where CFC rules in more than one jurisdiction apply to the same CFC income; and (iii) situations where a CFC actually distributes dividends out of income that has already been attributed to its resident shareholders under the CFC rules or a resident shareholder disposes of the shares in the CFC. However, double taxation concerns could arise in other situations, for instance where there has been a transfer pricing adjustment between two jurisdictions and a CFC charge arises in a third jurisdiction.[1] CFC rules should be designed to ensure that these and other situations do not lead to double taxation.

123. The recommendation for addressing the first two situations is to allow a credit for foreign taxes actually paid, including CFC tax assessed on intermediate companies. The actual tax paid (this can also include withholding taxes) should include all taxes borne by the CFC that are taxes on income that have not qualified for other relief, and that are not higher than the taxes due on the same income in the parent jurisdiction. The recommendation for addressing the third situation is to exempt dividends and gains on disposition of CFC shares from taxation if the income of the CFC has previously been subject to CFC taxation, but the precise treatment of such dividends and gains can be left to individual jurisdictions so that provisions are coherent with domestic law. It is left to individual jurisdictions to address other situations giving rise to double taxation, but the overall recommendation for this building block is to design CFC rules to ensure that they do not lead to double taxation.

7.2 Explanation

7.2.1 Issues with respect to relief for foreign corporate taxes

124. Perhaps the most obvious situation where the application of CFC rules may lead to double taxation is the one mentioned above under point (i) where the CFC income is subject to taxation in the CFC jurisdiction as well as to CFC taxation in the parent or controlling parties' jurisdiction.

125. Most jurisdictions address the situation where the CFC income is subject to taxation in both the CFC jurisdiction and the parent jurisdiction by providing for an indirect foreign tax credit that credits taxes that were incurred by a different taxpayer. This approach eliminates double taxation more comprehensively than the deduction method as it directly sets off the foreign tax against domestic tax rather than reducing the tax base to which the residence tax applies. Given that the purpose of a CFC regime is to assert taxing rights over income that has been shifted to another jurisdiction, the exemption method is not an appropriate method for granting relief in this context since it would undermine the application of CFC rules. An indirect foreign tax credit is generally limited to the amount of effective double taxation. This is addressed in most countries' rules by limiting relief to the lesser of the domestic tax or the foreign tax actually paid. The focus on the actual tax paid ensures that relief is not given if the foreign tax is subject to a refund or reimbursement claim. The actual tax paid (this can also include withholding taxes) should include all taxes borne by the CFC that are equivalent to taxes on income, that have not qualified for other relief, and that are not higher than the taxes due on the same income in the parent jurisdiction.

7.2.2 Issues with respect to relief for CFC taxation in multiple jurisdictions

126. Additional issues may arise when the income and profits arising in a CFC are taxed under the CFC rules operating in more than one jurisdiction, and this scenario may become more common in the future. If, for example, a subsidiary is treated as a CFC under the rules operating in multiple jurisdictions, then the subsidiary's income could potentially be taxed by the CFC jurisdiction and by any other jurisdiction that considers the subsidiary to be a CFC. Again an indirect foreign tax credit could be applied in this situation but in order to provide such a credit countries may need to change their double taxation relief provisions in order for CFC tax paid in an intermediate country to qualify as a foreign tax eligible for relief. There should also be a hierarchy of rules to determine which countries should have priority, and this hierarchy could prioritise the CFC rules of the jurisdiction whose resident shareholder is closer to the CFC in the chain of ownership.

127. This rule hierarchy is illustrated in Figure 7.1.

Figure 7.1 Interaction of CFC rules

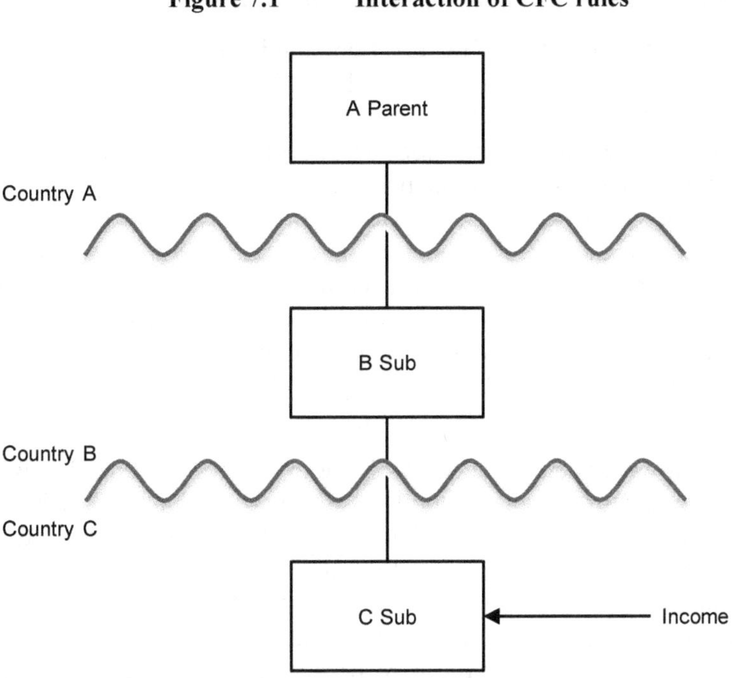

128. In this situation, C Sub is both a direct CFC of B Sub and an indirect CFC of A Parent, and B Sub is also a CFC of A Parent. If both Country A and Country B have CFC rules, there should be a rule hierarchy to determine which country's CFC rules will apply first.

129. Figure 7.1 could raise two different issues, depending on the tax rates of Country A and Country B. If Country C has a tax rate of 10%, Country B has a tax rate of 20%, and Country A has a tax rate of 30%, then both Country B and Country A will want to collect their full amount of tax, potentially only giving a credit for Country C's tax. If the income of C Sub is 100, this would mean that Country A would want to collect 20 (i.e., 30 minus 10) and Country B would want to collect 10 (i.e., 20 minus 10). The rule hierarchy suggested above, where Country B's rules apply prior to Country A's rules, would require that Country A provide a tax credit for taxes paid to both Country C and Country B. This would mean that Country C would collect 10, Country B would collect 10 (i.e., 20 minus 10), and Country A would also collect 10 (i.e., 30 minus 20)[2].

130. If, in contrast, Country C still has a tax rate of 10% and Country A still has a tax rate of 30%, but Country B has a tax rate of 40%, then Country A would no longer collect any taxes if it granted a tax credit for taxes paid to Country B. Although this may raise concerns from the perspective of Country A, this is likely to be consistent with the principle underlying Country A's CFC rules as C Sub would be fully taxed on its income at a tax rate greater than that in Country A. Also, if Country B has a tax rate that is higher than the tax rate in Country A, it is less likely that the tax base that has been eroded is that of Country A. It is more likely that in this situation, if it were to exist, it would be Country B's tax base that was being eroded. It would therefore be appropriate for Country A not to apply its CFC rules if the profits of C Sub are taxed at an equivalent or higher effective tax rate in the jurisdiction of an intermediate party. The recommended rule hierarchy in both situations is therefore for Country A to apply its CFC rules only after Country B has applied its CFC rules (or to provide a credit for CFC taxes paid to Country B, which may be simpler).

7.2.3 Relief for subsequent dividends and capital gains

131. The third situation in which CFC taxation could lead to double taxation is where (i) the CFC actually makes distributions out of the CFC income or (ii) resident taxpayers of a CFC dispose of their CFC shares. With regards to the first scenario, most jurisdictions provide some type of relief for subsequent dividends paid by a CFC. In the majority of these jurisdictions, the dividends will qualify for the regular participation exemption for foreign dividends. If CFC rules require a level of control that is at least equal to the same percentage of shareholding as the participation exemption, then the participation exemption is likely to apply. Therefore an additional relief provision will only be necessary if there is no participation exemption or the participation exemption does not apply. In these cases, most jurisdictions apply a separate provision that also exempts the dividends even if they do not qualify for the normal participation exemption (or if there is no general participation exemption).

132. There may however be difficulties with the exemption method if only part of the CFC income has been attributed to a resident taxpayer or if a CFC is indirectly held through another non-resident company which does not have attributable CFC income. In these cases it may be hard to determine whether dividends have, in fact, been paid out of attributed CFC income and are therefore subject to double taxation. To address these difficulties, countries tend to adopt relatively mechanical approaches that assume that dividends are likely to have been paid out of previously attributed CFC income. These approaches include, for example, limiting the dividend exemption to the amount of profits generated by the CFC during the tax years when CFC rules have applied.

133. A further issue that arises with regards to the first scenario occurs when the CFC jurisdiction applies withholding taxes when the dividend is paid out. Since these withholding taxes represent income taxation at the level of the CFC jurisdiction, it may be appropriate to provide relief for withholding taxes paid in respect of the CFC income.[3]

134. With regards to the second scenario, double taxation may also arise where the shares of a CFC are disposed of and the taxpayer holding the shares has previously been taxed on undistributed income of the CFC. Following the logic above in respect of dividends, countries may choose not to tax subsequent gains realised by a taxpayer in respect of the shares of a CFC to the extent that the same amounts have previously been taxed under CFC rules operating in the taxpayer's jurisdiction. However, given countries' different approaches to taxing gains on assets, the mechanism for providing relief is likely to vary to accommodate the specific tax features in each jurisdiction, and this recommendation does not mean that countries that do not otherwise exempt gains on disposition should change their overall rules to comply with this recommendation for CFC rules.

7.2.4 Other situations

135. The report recognises that double taxation can also arise in other ways, for instance through the interaction of CFC rules and transfer pricing rules. These are not new issues but countries will need to consider whether their existing double taxation relief provisions are effective in relieving all instances of double tax.[4]

7.2.5 Tax treaty provisions on the elimination of double taxation

136. The way in which a country should eliminate double taxation that may result from its CFC rules also needs to take account of that country's tax treaty obligations.

137. The elimination of double taxation found in bilateral tax treaties may vary considerably from the wording of Articles 23 A and 23 B of the *Model Tax Convention on Income and on Capital: Condensed Version* (OECD, 2010). States should therefore carefully review the relevant provisions of their tax treaties when designing their CFC regimes in order to make sure that they are not inadvertently required to apply the exemption method to income that they wish to tax under these regimes.

Notes

1. In certain circumstances, the interaction of CFC rules and transfer pricing rules could give rise to double taxation issues. Whilst such circumstances may not be common, it is important that countries rules contain provisions to eliminate any double taxation that would otherwise result.
2. This analysis assumes that Country A does not have a tax rate exemption or that the cut-off for Country A's tax rate exemption is greater than 20%.
3. The relief for withholding tax in a tax treaty situation is discussed in the Commentary of the *OECD Model Tax Convention* in paragraph 39 of Article 10.
4. For example, Parent A resident in Country A owns two subsidiaries, Sub B resident in Country B and Sub C resident in Country C. A transfer pricing adjustment is made between B and C resulting in higher profits in C. If Country A applies its CFC rules to both B and C it will need to give relief for the reduced foreign tax paid in B and the increased tax paid in C. In practice it seems more likely that where there are transfer pricing adjustments they will decrease the profits of a CFC and increase the profits of a more highly taxed subsidiary that is outside the scope of CFC rules. Therefore countries will need to be aware of any subsequent adjustments to the tax paid by a CFC to ensure that they do not provide relief for tax that has been repaid, and they should make it possible to reassess CFC taxation in similar situations even if the statute of limitation for such reassessments has passed.

Bibliography

OECD (2010), *Model Tax Convention on Income and on Capital: Condensed Version 2010*, OECD Publishing, Paris, http://dx.doi.org/10.1787/mtc_cond-2010-en.

ORGANISATION FOR ECONOMIC CO-OPERATION AND DEVELOPMENT

The OECD is a unique forum where governments work together to address the economic, social and environmental challenges of globalisation. The OECD is also at the forefront of efforts to understand and to help governments respond to new developments and concerns, such as corporate governance, the information economy and the challenges of an ageing population. The Organisation provides a setting where governments can compare policy experiences, seek answers to common problems, identify good practice and work to co-ordinate domestic and international policies.

The OECD member countries are: Australia, Austria, Belgium, Canada, Chile, the Czech Republic, Denmark, Estonia, Finland, France, Germany, Greece, Hungary, Iceland, Ireland, Israel, Italy, Japan, Korea, Luxembourg, Mexico, the Netherlands, New Zealand, Norway, Poland, Portugal, the Slovak Republic, Slovenia, Spain, Sweden, Switzerland, Turkey, the United Kingdom and the United States. The European Union takes part in the work of the OECD.

OECD Publishing disseminates widely the results of the Organisation's statistics gathering and research on economic, social and environmental issues, as well as the conventions, guidelines and standards agreed by its members.

OECD PUBLISHING, 2, rue André-Pascal, 75775 PARIS CEDEX 16
(23 2015 30 1 P) ISBN 978-92-64-24114-5 – 2015-01

www.ingramcontent.com/pod-product-compliance
Lightning Source LLC
LaVergne TN
LVHW081421110826
845149LV00010B/1832

9789264241145